ADIRONDACK PULP FICTION

To Lyn

For all her support and help

ADIRONDACK PULP FICTION

Larry Beahan

**Coyote Publishing of Western New York
5 Darwin Drive
Snyder New York 14226
larry_beahan@adelphia.net**

2006

Author Larry Beahan circa 1947

CONTENTS

PREFACE

In *Adirondack Pulp Fiction* you will find six tales of crime and passion. Despite what Chambers of Commerce and Adirondack Park authorities may claim, these human qualities do fire souls inside the Blue Line as well as out. The stories are not of lumberjack heroes, pioneers, hotel magnates, hermits or even mountain climbers. They are of ordinary people tangled in extraordinary emotions which lead them to extremes. These lives in backwaters, backwoods and mountain towns aren't just peaches and cream served up to you Little-House-on-the-Prairie style. You'll find very few log cabins with cheery fires and snug families in them.

These stories tell of the darker side of the hearts of Adirondack denizens. You already know of their good nature, hospitality and kindness now see the passion, envy, avarice and rage that dwell there too. Come stalk with me the slums, back roads, deserted mines, honky-tonks and gin-mills of Tupper Lake, Saranac Lake, Lake George, Lake Placid, Tahawus, North Creek, Gore Mountain and Fort Drum. Keep in mind, my good companions, these stories, like all fiction, have some basis in reality. Their events may have happened where we journey but, as far as I know, they did not.

Larry Beahan, November 11, 2006

TRIXIE IN HER TRACKS

In the old days, George Therett and Papa worked together cutting timber in the Independence River country. Later Mister Therett had a dairy farm and needed another hired man. Papa thought I could learn a thing or two off him and bring in a few dollars at the same time. I was done with school and too young for the pulp mill so it sounded like a pretty good idea to me, too.

      It was chilly that November in 1921. I was sixteen. Mister Therett had me hauling milk ten miles to the Antwerp milk station, which I didn't mind at all. He had two teams for doing the hauling and he let me have the Grays. They were a dandy pair. Called them Duke and Duchess. He taught me how to hitch them up and drive them, even let me plow with them. I felt pretty important sitting behind those two big horses pulling a half ton of milk to market every day. He had the contract to haul milk to Antwerp for all the farms up that way in the cold weather, October to May. In the summer individual farmers hauled their own milk to the cheese factory.

Missus Therett taught school so she had a hired girl.

They had 300 acres, a nice big house, good barn and me and
Alton Jonas for hired men. We all lived in their big house on
the Antwerp Road. It was just eight miles from my home in

Carthage and not far from Pine Plains where Momma used to talk about going after blueberries when she was a kid. Army took over a lot of the Plains in 1908 for a training camp. Eventually built Fort Drum there.

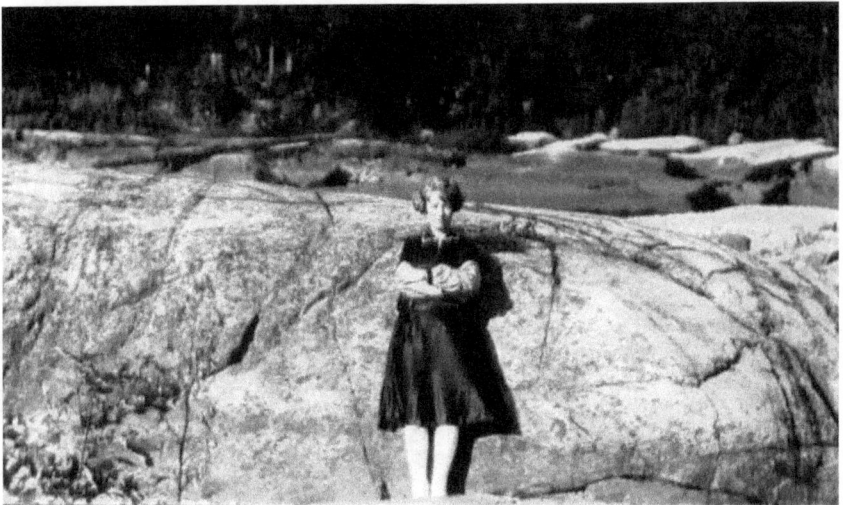

Alma was the hired girl, Mike Collins' oldest daughter from two miles up the Antwerp Road. She did most of the cooking and some milking. She was a pretty good cook and kind of sweet on me. Momma warned me to look out for her since she was older. We did a little smooching but it didn't amount to too much. At least I didn't think so.

When this all happened, Prohibition had been in force over a year and everyone was talking about bootleggers with their fast cars, fast women and rum-runnin' speed boats. Mister Therett said Prohibition got people to drinking more 'cause, now, they weren't supposed to drink at all and how unreasonable the Volstead Act was and how he was even tempted to set up a still back of his sugar bush and run off some moonshine himself.

I'd been working for Therett a year, making five dollars a week with no expenses to speak of. So I was feeling pretty flush. I took some money home to Momma and I took some to buy myself this big sheepskin coat. I figured I'd wear it while I was driving the horses to town but there was so much work to loading and unloading I hardly ever got a chance to get cold. Spent more time sitting on that coat than ever wearing it.

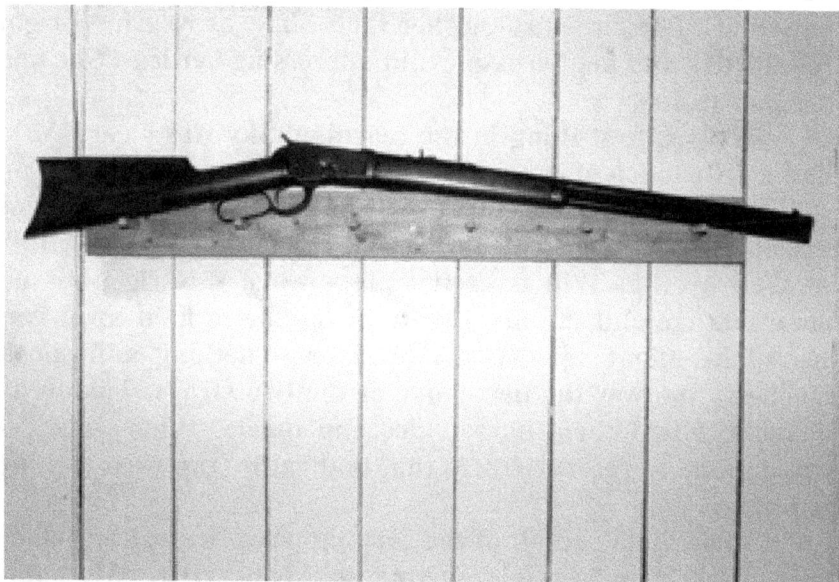

And I bought a rifle. Alton Jonas and I went hunting over there toward Indian River a few weeks before this happened. Mister Therett gave me the day off and loaned me an old 22 of his.

Alton and I didn't see much worth shooting at but we had a nice hike and we roasted some potatoes in a fire. We stopped in to see old Johnnie Jones. Had a cabin up that way, batchin' it on his own. He gave us some coffee and he talked a lot about old times. Complained he was too crippled-up to hunt anymore. Showed us this dandy Winchester model 1898 lever-action deer rifle he had.

I asked him, "What will you take for it?" Never thought he'd give it up. He let me have it for eight dollars. I took to carrying it on the milk wagon. Thought I might see a deer some time.

What I did finally see was a fancy dude in a big sky-blue color sedan. I had never seen an automobile quite so big as the one he had. Dude was wearing a fedora hat and big black overcoat and he was puffing on a cigarette. A real pretty girl was in the seat alongside him. She had on a fur coat made out of about 20 good-sized raccoons and one of these tight-fit hats that come close around her face. She was wearing bright red lipstick and kept crossing and uncrossing her legs. She had a cigarette, too.

It was first thing in the morning. Sky was clear. We'd had a little touch of snow. The water on our pond had froze up solid and you could see your breath in the air. I had just come out of the barn with the horses and started for my first milk pick-up over to Will Everett's place when this rig pulls up alongside me and the dude motions for me to hold up. I was scared he might squawk the horn or something and spook Duchess. She was the nervy one of the two Grays. Taking no chances, I told them horses nice and quiet, "Whooa-up." I eased on up to reassure them that that rattle trap wasn't going to bite.

The dude got out of the car, big fellow he was and dark hair. "Hello Son," he said, poking out his big paw, "My name is Ike Spencer and this here is my girl Trixie." He motioned for her to get out of the car.

The girl got out of the other side of the car and came around to where we were standing. She had on high heels that made the gravel road hard going.

I said, "Hi, pleased to meet you. I'm Tom Kelley. Work for Mister George Therett here," and I motioned toward the house. I shook hands with him. He had a hard shake for a city fella'. He pulled me in close to him and stared hard at me with one of the toughest looking looks I ever seen. Trixie surprised me, too. She put out a little soft hand to shake and she let her coat hang open.   I believe she was stark staring naked underneath. Either that or she was all dressed in pink.

The two of them kind of took me back and I guess they could see that. He said, "Nice and warm in that Caddy. They put heaters in them, you know."

She smiled at me and winked. And boy, could she wink.

Ike said, "Now Son, we're strangers around here and we're looking for a way up to Alexandria Bay. Want to meet some friends up that way. Figure'd you could help us."

"Well, well sure, you just take this road here up to Antwerp," I started out.

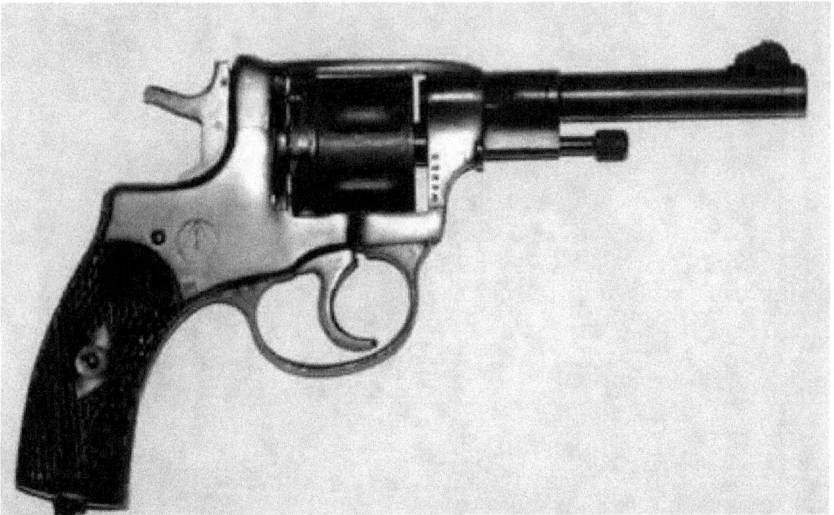

He gave me a push on the shoulder that set me back a step and he laughed, "No, that's why we stopped you. We're looking for some back way to get past Antwerp. We're trying to avoid the big towns."

Trixie was standing dangerously close to me, I thought. Danger of what, I didn't know. She said, "Tommie, that's your name, ain't it?" I gulped and nodded. "Tommie, I got to tell you something Ike's not tellin'. Ike, here, is a bootlegger and he don't want your sheriff to know he's running through this territory."

Ike pulled up a stalk of timothy from the side of the road and tickled her with the end of it, "Trixie, I'm going to have to cut you off your hooch. You talk too much."

"It's like this," Ike said. "I'm in the import business. And I have to pick up some stock that a friend of mine is bringing across the Saint Lawrence River in a motor boat. He's doing it at great risk and I don't want to fail him. Now we all know there is some disagreement whether liquor -- and this is this high-quality Scotch liquor -- whether it requires a government stamp on it. I prefer to avoid the controversy by using a few back roads. I'm hoping you see it my way and are willin' to help out."

"Own up to the truth now, Honey; tell the man, that Antwerp sheriff stopped your shipment last week." Trixie said this in that teasing big-city style of hers, winking and pushing a furry hip into Ike so I got a look at a lot of leg where the coonskins kind of parted.

The *Carthage Republican* had a front page story about Ike's lost shipment. Mister Therett showed it to me. In fact, he went to town and bought a quart of the confiscated goods. Said it weren't no better nor much worse than some that had been made around here. So I was way ahead of these two on that one. I just nodded and said, "Uh huh," as I eased away from Trixie and tried to get a look into the fancy car.

She kind of followed along saying, "Take a good look, Honey." I think she called everyone "Honey" once she heard their Christian name. "All mohair interior, solid cherry dashboard and good hooch in that little compartment there. You want a little something?" She licked her lips suggestive of, I don't know for sure what.

I took it all in plus I saw a big western six-shooter pistol in a holster strapped to the steering column. Trixie said, "Oh, that's in case we run into bad guys. I bet you've got a pretty nice gun, too," she crooned and nuzzled close to me.

Oh my, where is this going? I thought and I looked over my shoulder. Sure enough, there was Alma staring out the front window at us. Oh my God!

But Ike was looking, too, "Now you let him alone Trixie, none of your teasing," he laughed. "So, young fella', you gonna' help us out? You know any way we can by-pass Antwerp?"

I wasn't sure what to make of this. Here was a real live bootlegger and a gun moll, like in the newspapers. They were armed and making a run for it, after booze. And they wanted me to help out. Seemed like my life was moving faster than I planned. I just hired out to learn farming and here I am getting swept into the rackets. Better slow down.

I said, "Maybe there is, but you best talk to Mister Therett about that. He knows this country a lot better than I do." Alma must have told everyone what was going on because Therett had gotten up from his bacon and eggs before he could have finished and he was headed down the drive with his big fur hat pulled partway on and his lumber jacket hanging open.

I introduced them. "Mister Therett, this here is Ike Spencer, and this is Trixie. Folks, this is George Therett, owns this place."

Therett was just as big a man as Ike and when they shook hands I could see they was sizin' each other up. I explained the predicament. Which Ike went and explained all over again. At first Mister Therett acted like he would rather have stayed in and et his whole breakfast, the way he kind of looked funny at me, but when he caught on to the deal, he was cordial enough to them.

"So you got to get to Alex Bay, he said, "and you don't want to bump into Luke Evans, our Sheriff, huh. Can't blame you. He's a mean old son-of-a-bitch. That's why I voted for him. But he's got no choice about you. No matter what his philosophy is on Prohibition laws. He's got to enforce them. If he expects you're comin' through town, he'll stop you for sure."

Ike was smiling like he knew he was going to get help and Trixie was dancing from one foot to another like she needed to use our backhouse which I would have been glad to show her. But Mister Therett said, "Tommie, you best be getting on your way. Don't want to get that milk into the station late. It's got to be ready for the four o'clock train."

I tipped my hat to them all and backed away toward the horses. Wanted to kind of let the horses know everything was

OK and it was time we got to work. Ike said, "Much obliged, Son, for your help."

But Trixie followed right along with me. "Tommie, Honey, I love horses. Can I pet them before you go?"

What could I say? So we went up and I gave Duchess a little pat saying, "This one here is Duchess and that there is Duke."

"Oh, can I pet him?"

"Sure, just be careful, move slow and let him smell you." Ehm, she did smell good, had on some kind of perfume. So she give Duke a little pat and he snuffled her some. Then she said, "Tommie, Honey, could you give me a drink of milk. I'm thirsty and I'm starving. Ike don't want to stop for nothin' when he's doin' business."

I didn't now how Mister Therett would take it but I decided I'd take a chance, she asked so nice. I quick swung up on the wagon, pulled the lid off a 20-gallon-milk can and scooped her a scooper full of nice creamy top-milk.

She took it and tilted it into her mouth, smiling. I don't think she was too used to drinkin' out of a scooper 'cause she dribbled down one side of her mouth but she didn't care. She took it down all in one big swallow. When she came up to breathe I was back alongside her and she leaned over on to me. Gave me the biggest creamiest kiss on the mouth I ever had. Then she said, "Tommie, Honey, that is so good. Just like my daddy used to bring us home when he went fishin' out in the country. Thank you so--o much."

I think she might have just gone on kissin' but Ike seen what happened. He yelled over, "Trixie, get your keister back in that car. Then he looked at me with them hard eyes, "Watch yourself, Kiddo."

What a day, I never expected to be kissed like that or to be threatened by a gangster. I didn't know what to do but get up on the wagon and skedaddle before anything else happened.

The rest of the morning was pretty uneventful by comparison. I collected all my milk cans and carried them up to the station in Antwerp. I didn't see any police barricading the roads waiting for bootleggers or outlaws. I thought maybe Ike Spencer was exaggerating.

I got back to Therett's, put the team in their stalls, gave them hay and water and a good rubdown and headed in the house to wash up for supper. Oh my! I didn't know what I was in for. I went to get some hot water out of the tank behind the stove and Alma blocked my way. "You don't need no hot water. What you need is a cold shower."

"Cold shower, what do you mean?"

"I seen you with that neked city girl. I seen you give away our milk to her so she'd kiss you."

"She was thirsty and hungry. She wasn't naked. She had a coat on."

"You gave her our milk and, the Hussy; she climbed all over you, Tommie, without a stitch on. I don't ever want anything to do with you no more. Go on out to the pump if you want water and you better wash up pretty good after that. I saw the whole thing."

"Alma, Honey---"

"Don't you Honey me. Go on, get on out of here. Wash up in the barn. Dinner ain't ready yet." This last she was shouting as she bum-rushed me out the kitchen door into the barnyard.

I went over to the barn. Shep, Therret's big mutt, came over wanting a scratch and I gave it to him. He lay down in the sun and rolled over begging for a belly rub, too. Mister Therett and Alton were there just finishing up the afternoon milking. Alton came on razzing me. "You're in trouble now. Think you can two-time Alma? Wait till her old man hears about this. Wahoo", he yelled and threw a bunch of hay at me.

"Lay off, Alton, or you'll be eating a knuckle sandwich," I told him

Then Mister Therett said, "Pretty funny this morning, your city girl friend was sitting in the backhouse and your buddy, here, sneaks up behind and yells, 'Ma'm, would you mind moving over to the next hole. I'm working down here.' You should have seen her come running out of there, coonskins flapping in the breeze.'"

I was surprised at Mister Therett. I thought that old joke was kind of mean, but who was I to say. So I let it pass. Besides, just then who comes dragging in the yard but that dude, Ike Spencer. He's still got on that fedora hat but he's carrying his big coat on one arm. We walked over toward him. He stopped, squinted, took off the hat and wiped sweat from his bald head. The day had warmed considerably. The ice on our pond was gone.

"Howdy there Mister Spencer," said Mister Therett. "You look like you had a hard day. Get your business done?" Therett was chewing on a piece of straw

Alton kind of hung back but I said, "Hello, Ike." We kind of let Mister Therett take care of business.

"Got a real mess. That old road you showed me worked fine this morning. Zipped right on through over some icy patches. Coming back the ice was gone. Now we are in the muck up over our hubs. We're back in there half mile or so from the main road. Trixie's sitting there with my old 45 guarding the hooch."

"Don't say I didn't warn you this morning," said Mister Therett. "I told you that meadow road would soften up this afternoon."

Mister Therett had his own opinions about alcoholic beverages and so did I but somehow I never thought it of him that he'd go into business with a shady character like Ike Spencer. I figured we were all dead meat, if Sheriff Evans showed up just now.

"It was that or run a damn road block. That old Caddy with its 79 horse V 8 has never failed me before."

"Seventy-nine horses you say, huh, I got a pair of Grays here that are better than any V 8 ever made when it comes to getting out of muck."

"Bring 'em on then. Let's see what they can do."

"What's it worth to you, Mister?" said Mister Therett, chewing away at his straw.

"So that's how it is. You get me stuck in there and now you want to hold me up for a bunch of money, you hick bastard. You know who you're trying to bamboozle? Maybe you never heard of Bugs Malloy down at Rochester."

Ike was a big man and he was making like he was going to throw down his coat and roll up his sleeves, John L. Sullivan style. But old Mister Therett had been through some lumber camp brawls, to hear him tell it, and he was a cool one. He knew he had Ike in a pickle.

"Take it easy, Ike. Don't want to hold you up but you want to use my team, I got to charge you something. You got you a nice car, fancy girl friend and a load of scotch. I'll be glad to help you out, for a reasonable consideration."

"I'll give you ten dollars. But get those damned old nags out of the barn and let's get a move on."

"Make it thirty."

"You fucking bandits!" Ike yelled pulling a twenty-dollar Greenback out of his wallet. "Twenty bucks and if that's not enough, we'll be back here and you'll wish you had done it for free."

"Deal!" said Mister Therett sweeping the Greenback out of the dude's fist and into his coverall pocket.

He and I headed to the barn. Alton took Ike over to the pump and pumped him a dipper of water. Ike drank a dipper full and then leaned over and poured another one on his shiny dome. Then he jabbed a finger at Alton and laughed menacingly. "You're some joker, ain't you kid. Funny guy. Huh?"

Alton backed away kind of sheepish like. Maybe he learned himself a thing or two about messin' with a sweet thing like Trixie.

In the barn, Duchess really protested when I got her up and started laying harness on her again. But Duke stepped in beside her and she calmed down. I found them a couple of apples each and that mended their spirits some. We hitched up a light wagon That Mister Therett used for going to town. While we were doing that Mister Therett nudged me and whispered, "Put that new rifle of yours in the wagon box. It's loaded, ain't it?" I nodded.

Alma came out of the house to see what was going on. She and Mister Therett had their heads together for quite a spell and he finally shook his head no and sent her back in the house. He said to me, "Damn fool girl wants to come along and make sure there's no monkey business with that Trixie gal. Don't know what's wrong with her. The Collins's have always been good solid folks."

I shrugged.

Mister Therett drove the horses and he had that Ike dude sit up beside him. Alton and I got in the wagon box behind them and we bumped our way down the old road that began in one corner of Therett's place and headed north connecting with some other seldom-used roads. The trace went through a bit of second growth, around a rocky outcrop, down a hill, forded a narrow brook and entered a meadow. We found the Cadillac, its sky-blue body plastered with mud and the whole car deep in a section of beaver-flooded meadow where there was barely a trace of road anymore.

Ike was belaboring the point. "By rights you should have told me no one has been through here in years. It's more of a damn horse path than a God damn auto road. You should have warned me."

"Look Mister, it was you who was so eager to get through here. I didn't stop you on the road and tell you where to go. Come to think of it, I should have told you to go straight to hell."

I wanted to tell them to just ease up and get the car out of there. I was thinking about how we were all going to split up that twenty dollars and maybe a bottle of scotch. But they simmered down on their own.

Trixie was sound asleep in the front seat of the Cadillac. Her arms were crossed and the six shooter in her one hand pointed out the window. Ike motioned us to be quiet and whispered, "Don't want to startle a lady with her finger on the trigger of gun." We nodded and he started wading over toward her though the muck. Some flies were bothering Duchess so she was swishing her tail around. I climbed down to go up and pat her.

Then Trixie brushed a fly off her nose without even opening an eye. Alton giggled, and gave me a silent hee-haw. He must've thought it was funny seeing Duchess and Trixie drawing flies.

Ike stepped into a hole and staggered for a second reaching over into the water to catch his balance and getting his shirt and jacket soaked. Trixie must have heard the splash and she jerked upright. The 45 went off with a bang that echoed in the silence half way to Antwerp. I lost Trixie behind a puff of smoke for a second but I saw Ike go down with a hand to the left side of his chest. He slid partway down into the muck gurgling, coughed and was silent.

I got aholt of Duchess' halter to keep her from bolting, but she was up in the air a couple of times before I had her calmed down.

Trixie came clear from behind the smoke, yelling. She didn't seem to realize right away what happened. "Where the hell you stiffs been? It's scary sitting out here in the woods! I saw a bear!"

Mister Therett made his way toward her. "Take it easy, Honey. Put the gun down. Looks like Ike is hurt. Let me see how he is."

"I'm keeping the gun," she said pointing it straight at him and cocking it again.

"OK, OK," said Mister Therett backing off. "What do you want us to do?'

Trixie brushed her blond hair back with her free hand. She looked out the window at Ike laying still in the mud, blood oozing about him. I'm not sure but I think there might have been a tear in the corner of her eye. "Looks like he's a goner. The stupid son of a bitch. I told him never to sneak up on me. I got a hair-trigger. God damn it!"

"We'll pull you out," Mister Therett called. "It was an accident. Not your fault. Put the damn gun down. Makes me nervous."

I helped unhitch Duke and Duchess from the wagon and got them turned around so Alton could get a chain around the front axle.

Mister Therett called to Trixie, "Do you want me to take a look at Ike? He might be alive yet."

Trixie had never taken the gun off Therett the whole time. She said, "Just get me the fuck out of this hole or I'll blow you away, too."

Duke and Duchess gave a mighty heave but it barely lurched the big machine.

"God damn it," said Mister Therett, "we're going to have to push."

Hearing that, Trixie climbed out of the car in her bare feet waving the pistol, the tails of her coat dragging in the mud as she waded over to dry ground. She looked shaky and scared even though she was cussin' like a trooper, "Get that fucking car moving, you sons-of-bitches. Get me the hell out of here, God damn you!"

Mister Therett said, "Tommie, you got more beef on you, come on in here and help me push. Alton can manage the team." With Duchess upset already, I didn't trust Alton to handle her so I hesitated.

Mister Therett was getting nervous and he yelled at me, first time he ever did that. "Tommie, God damn it, get over here." Trixie saw that I was holding back so she put the gun up in the air and fired again. Bang! Bang! Duchess started going nuts and I held on to her for dear life. Every time Duchess and me came down out of the air I could see Trixie trying to draw a bead on me.

That must have been what made Alma rise up in the box of the wagon. I don't know how she got there so quiet. She must have followed us and snuck in there while we were worrying about everything else. She had my Winchester up to her shoulder pointed at Trixie. I started toward her. "No, no, don't--"

Alma yelled, "Jezebel!"

The rifle went off, "Blam, blam, blam." Poor Trixie looked at me kind of surprised and hurt. Then she dropped in her tracks.

There's not much else to tell.

Mister Therett said, "They were strangers and they brought it on themselves. Alma done right. That girl had the drop on us."

I thought Alma maybe overreacted, but who knows what Trixie might have done. "I told Alma, 'You saved our lives'."

She was pretty tore up about it at first. She kept on sayin' things like, "I only meant to wing her. That's all I meant. I thought she was going to kill all of you."

We tucked Ike and Trixie in the back seat of that big old Caddy. Last time I went into Therett's back pasture, beavers had raised that dam so that you had to look real careful and still all you could see of the Caddy was kind of a rusty shadow under the dark water of the pond. The whiskey, we brought up to the barn and it lasted a good while.

I wound up with Alma. On our anniversary we share a milk scoop of scotch whiskey together and think on what happened to Trixie and Ike.

All that hassle and Therett never split the twenty with Alton and me.

CHERRY PIE

A woman stepped out on the porch of the cabin a few feet away. Her gleaming black hair was long, her lips, painted flaming red and her body was more voluptuously conformed than any girl of my tender experience. I caught the scent of jasmine.

I was twenty-one. She was a tad older, maybe twenty-six. We were both moving into tiny staff cabins at Lake George Beach. Mine was two rooms and a porch covered with spider webs but it was my very own, my first bachelor pad.

She smiled stepping toward me with an undulant sway. Her movement mocked that of the graceful hemlock overhead swaying in a June Adirondack breeze. My pulse leapt as I imagined what impelled those hips. "Hel...lo there," she hailed across the little stretch of sand dividing our cottages. She let the hel...lo roll out languidly as if it were a pronunciation that

she had devised especially for me.
  "Hi," I gulped.
  She cocked a smile.

I swallowed, "You need help carrying stuff up from your car?"

"No thanks. We're old hands here, our fifth summer. This must be your first."

Before I could answer, the screen door screeched open behind her and a chubby, gray-headed, shorter version pushed through. "Josephine," she croaked "he could bring up the ice!"

"Ma, I said I'd get it. We should at least introduce ourselves before we put him to work" and turning to me, "I am Josephine, Queen of the Lake George Bathhouse." Then she posed, raising both hands to brush back her hair. The sight of those breasts forcing themselves to mold the blue chambray shirt arrested me, mouth agape. I could see points…nipples! Her shirt-tails were outside her white jeans and knotted about her waist to reveal flesh in V's beneath and above those succulent orbs… and a comely bellybutton.

Mrs. Lombardo scowled disapproval. But Josephine did not quickly surrender the power of that simple gesture that had enslaved me.

"This is my mother, Mrs. Lombardo. You are...?"

"I'm Charlie Hanks. I'm the lifeguard." I gave Mrs. Lombardo a quick grin, "Please let me get the ice for you." I stepped off my front porch toward the parking lot, my eyes fixed on Josephine.

"Thanks. That ice is heavy for a woman to carry. Careful you don't squash my cherries. I got cherries in the trunk by the ice...for a pie," shouted Mrs. Lombardo.

That afternoon we opened the beach but had few visitors. I sat on a bench in the warm sun in front of the bathhouse. The wind had whipped up some chop on the lake. No one was in the water so I opened a copy of D.H. Lawrence's "Lady Chatterley's Lover." Absorbed by one section that fit my own ideas so well, I did not immediately react to a tickle at the back of my neck. When I slapped at it, I grabbed a whisk of elephant grass instead of a bug.

Josephine, wielding it, laughed, "What are you reading? Aren't you supposed to watch in case somebody drowns?"

She sat close beside me and took the book out of my hands. "Oh, 'Lady Chatterley's Lover.'" She nudged me with a hip, "You're too young for that. Let me have it. I'm all out of stuff to read."

I sat up, tilted my Yankee's cap rakishly toward her and said, "No, I'm right in the middle of the good part."

Before I could react, Josephine slipped me that crooked smile of hers and dashed abruptly into the women's locker room ... my book in her hand.

For half an hour, I made do, skipping flat stones on the water with one of the other guards. I was bored. So I barged into the women's locker room, first calling in a disarming tone, "Yoo-hoo, everybody decent?"

"Stay out. This is private," Josephine screamed in mock alarm. She was alone, perched on a counter, her back against a wall, bare knees pulled up against her chest. Short red shorts creased her enticing thighs while her eyes bored deep into my book.

"Josephine, I want my book"

"Mmm," she groaned.

"Give it to me, please." I said.

"Mmm hmm."

"Give it to me...or else."

"Or else what?" she answered looking up for the first time.

"Or else...," my mind searched for a consequence, "I'll tickle you?"

Her languorous eyes appraised me and she gave a knowing smile. "This is a go...od book," she said low and husky, extending the good in a way I was almost sure she had never done for anyone else. As she stretched and yawned, I was stunned by the lazy sensual excitement she exuded.

Then she grasped my little paperback book with those graceful scarlet-nailed fingers and worked its spine back and forth. She massaged and tormented those fortunate pages so smoothly, so caressingly, that I felt myself melting like butter in summer sun, no...stiffening... in envy. In a final surge she tore the book down the middle and said, "Here, you take half."

Her disregard for the sanctity of books hit me. What else was she capable of, perhaps the Full Monty, the whole shebang, maybe a home run? I took my half of the book in a perspiring hand and faded back into the open air of the lakefront. My breath came easier. I read with half an eye on the beach and half on the door that concealed Josephine. Waves surged against the beach as mountains peered knowingly across the lake at me. But nothing disturbed my recasting of D. H. Lawrence's passionate fantasies with my own "Lady of the Locker Room and her Lifeguard."

In the afternoon the wind came up and the beach took a wonderful pounding from surf. We beach staff had the park to ourselves. I found a wooden plank for belly surfing and had a great time riding the waves. Josephine came out of her locker room wrapped in a flaming orange and yellow beach towel. She posed, head held high, hair streaming in the wind. She watched me.

"Charlie, how do you do that?" she called over the wind.

"I'll take you for a ride if you take me home for a piece of that cherry pie."

"Sorry, Charlie, Momma doesn't feed lifeguards."

"I'm sorry, too. You'd get a kick out of this," and I launched myself and my plank out into the surf. I'd show her something. I waited for a big curling wave. I catapulted off the bottom and caught it for the longest and what I hoped would be the second most satisfying ride of the day. Eat your heart out, Josie Baby.

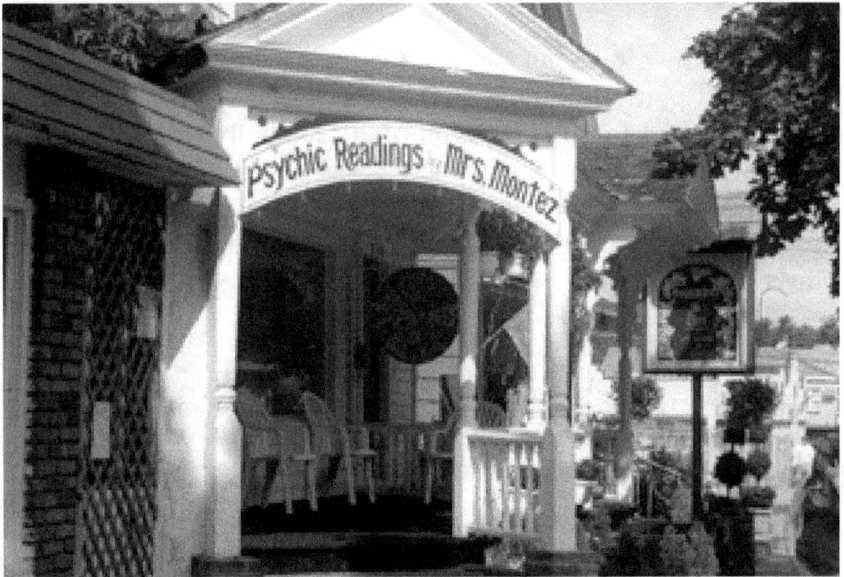

I glided in majestically at her feet.

"You want to try?" I asked.

She hesitated.

"Come on, I'll give you a ride."

"How?" She unwrapped her towel and let it slip to the sand, revealing a black and orange bikini that just contained her. She reached for my hand and I led her into the surf. I imagined the power of the waves tugging at the fastenings of that tiny suit and I cheered them on.

"You lay on the board and when a big wave looks like it will break near us you push off the bottom and throw yourself on to it," I instructed.

"I can't do that."

"Well then, let me stand right behind you and jump on with you," I offered.

She looked at me a moment and said, "No, no, that won't work either."

Finally I said, "You get behind me. I'll catch the wave and you jump on top of me." She said, "OK, I'll try that."

She huddled up close behind me. I got into position, picked out a good wave and counted, "One, two, three. Go." And we were off on a surging wave and me with all of that wonderful woman caressing my back. Oh, if I had hands on my back. God, I could have done that all day but then Momma Lombardo showed up on the beach.

"Josephine, come here, you wanna' get drownded," she yelled. "Your supper is ready."

"I'm coming, Momma."

"Hurry it up, honey. I got to go home tonight. Auntie Angie is sick."

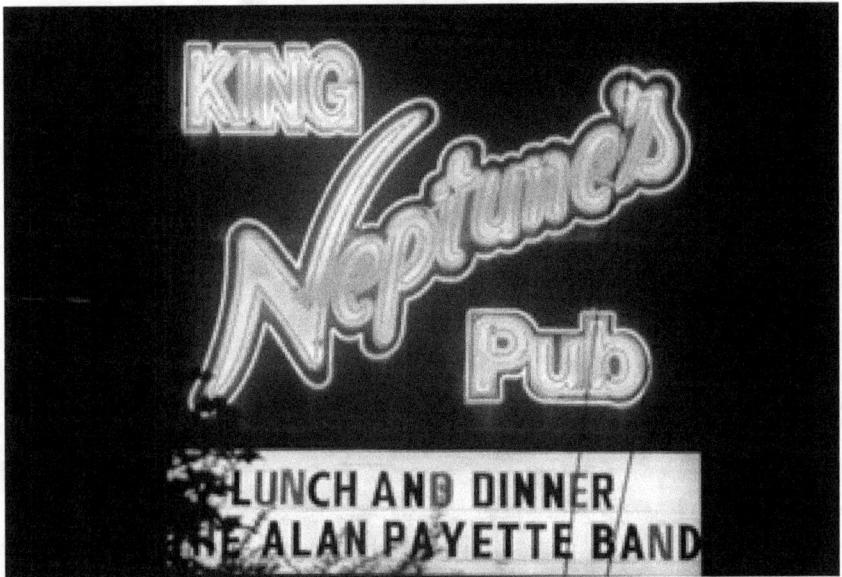

Momma disappeared. Josephine dried herself and then offered me her towel. I used it and finished off burying my head in tufts redolent of Josephine. Jasmine floated about us. She wound the towel around herself and we walked toward our cabins.

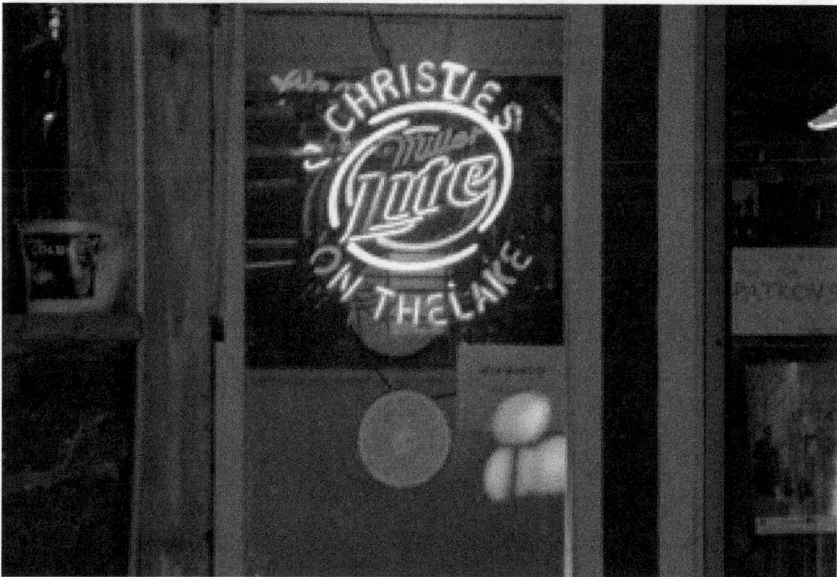

"Josephine," I said, "How about a stroll up the Boardwalk tonight. *The Heaters* are playing at King Neptune's."

"Oh, I'm so sorry. No, I can't. I've got a date."

What a disappointment, what bad news. I'm sure these feelings were written across my face because she repeated, "I am sorry. She's an old friend and this has been set up for a long time."

She? I thought. Who is she?

"Her family has a place at Bolton Landing. She and her brother and I, we used to hang out." Josephine paused for a moment and added, "Why don't you come along? It might be interesting."

Me on a date with two girls? Now that didn't sound so bad.

"Yeah, yeah, what are you going to do? I mean, yes, sure, I'd love to."

"We're going to meet about eight, maybe get a slice at Soprano's or some of that sausage they cook down at the beach, have a couple of drinks and go somewhere to dance."

"Sounds great. Thanks," I said. That smile of Josephine's was so inviting. I leaned over to give her a peck on the cheek. She dodged, deftly brushing me with the soft contents of that blue chambray shirt.

That night, Josephine asked me to drive her old Chevy convertible for her. We put the top down and cruised down 9N past mansions, Honky-Tonks and cottages to an ice cream stand. There we found Patsy leaning against her red pick-up.

She was a tall, slim, athletic girl dressed in jeans, cowboy boots and a western shirt. With a whooping "Howdy" she rushed over to hug Josephine. Then she came to the driver's side and said, "Hi Stranger. Slide over. I know these parts better than you." I surrendered the wheel and squeezed pleasurably over against Josephine. Patsy slammed down the gas pedal and off we screeched.

At Ray's Helova Deli, Patsy paid our tab before either Josephine or I had a chance. She poured an extra dose of hot sauce on her sausage and inhaled it before either of us were half through ours. Winking at Josephine and massaging the bare flesh of Josephine's lower back she said, "Mmm, turns on the fires inside, don't it?"

"Mmm, humm, very hot," Josephine crooned over her sausage.

At the Adirondack Pub and Brewery, after trying a couple of different home-made brews, I led them in singing, "The Lady in Red." I really laid the part on them that goes,

"Her mother never told her
The things a young girl should know
About the ways of college men
And how they come and go
...mostly come."

We all laughed, then Patsy gave a rendition of "Lil," that went,

"From out of the hills around Drag Ass Creek
Came a sawed-off pimp called Piss Pot Pete"

Except Patsy knew astounding verses to it that I had never heard. The same with dirty stories.

I tried bragging about long distance swimming. That was a mistake because she claimed she swam across the whole lake once.

We wound up on Josephine's front porch.

"Look at that moon," Josephine said. "Isn't it romantic?"

I had been holding Josephine's hand but Patsy took it from me and said looking at her, "This has been such a wonderful evening."

To myself, I agreed it had been promising to be wonderful but how to get rid of this Patsy?

I tried to regain the hand that I lost and found Josephine giving me her other hand instead. Patsy and I stood there staring at sweet Josephine as she smiled sublimely at the moon.

"It's getting late," Josephine whispered.

"I'd love some cherry pie," I whispered back.

"No, no, Momma's saving that."

"How about a good night kiss, then ?

Josephine laughed deep down in her throat and nodded.

Patsy raised an eyebrow and leaned away.

I enfolded that lovely body of Josephine's in my arms. But with one hand she still clung to Patsy. The kiss did not go well. Josephine seemed awkward, nothing like that molten woman on my back when we rode the surf. As I kissed her, her lips parted. I could not get a decent seal. I was losing her.

Yet, when I let Josephine go, Patsy had lost her composure. She seemed almost tearful. They held each other at arms length, looked into each others eyes, then softly embraced. I could see Josephine's mouth opened as Patsy covered it with hers. They twisted away from me. Josephine dropped my hand.

My heart sank.

When at last they broke off, Josephine whispered, "Thanks Charlie." And the two of them disappeared through that noisy screen door leaving me only the scent of jasmine and the image of Patsy's hand sliding down Josephine's bare back.

In the dark, I lay on my cot next door, tormented by Patsy's giggles. After a seemingly endless hour, I heard the screen door screech and slam, then only crickets and the lapping of waves until Josephine's whisper undulated across our narrow divide. "Charlie would you like a little...cherry pie?"

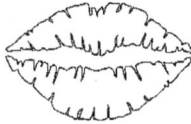

TUPPER SANTA

On a back street near the railroad tracks in lower Tupper Lake a light glared from one of two second-story windows in an old frame house. It was snowing lightly that Christmas Eve. The only decoration in the window was a partially drawn shade, its circular pull dangling. The window frame had been painted many times. Its checkered paint was badly chipped. Inside, curly-haired brown-eyed Susie sat huddled over a hot water radiator as she stared out watching snow soften the contours of Adirondack poverty.

Behind her, Brian had been whimpering quietly in front of the television for a long, long time. His alligator program interrupted for a Coca Cola commercial and he broke off to complain, "I'm hungry." The four-year-old with the runny nose and weepy eyes turned up the pitch and wailed, "Wake momma up. Want my oatmeal. She gotta' git up."

Susie, weighed down by her two years of seniority, started toward him but out in the street a wounded beast of an old Buick missing a headlight grabbed her attention. Snowflakes lit up like tiny feathers in the beam cast by its single eye as it crept to a stop in front of their shabby house. Her heart sank. Two teen-age boys in oversized hooded sweatshirts and nylon baseball jackets hurried into the alley and slammed the back door as they entered the flat beneath Brian and Susie. "It's Mikey and Peter. One of their headlights gone out," she said to Brian. "Wished it was Santa...or the pizza man."

The two runaway boys had moved in downstairs when the previous tenant went to jail on a burglary charge. So far the absentee landlord had not learned of these impromptu arrangements.

Susie, in her raveled purple sweater, turned again toward her charge. She put a forefinger to her lips and hissed, "Shhhhh," then went to him and laid an arm around the little boy's shoulders. "Momma need her rest. She just stop coughing." Susie smoothed Brian's red hair and tucked his soiled sweatshirt into the elastic band of his dungarees. "There's a little more flour. How 'bout I make some bap?"

Brian wiped his nose on his sleeve and looked up at Susie, adoring now instead of angry. "Can I help?"

"Sure can. You can stir." They stood up from the worn carpet. Susie turned off the television. The people at the Social Services building had not included a remote when, in better days, their mother had lovingly procured the children's constant companion from them. That day had been wonderful. Their mother wasn't sick and social service gave them a free pass to the Wild Center. They remembered all the fish swimming around, "right in front of you." The back-flipping river otter still made them laugh when they thought of him.

In the kitchen Susie used a stepstool to retrieve a sauce pan and a spoon from the sink where several other partially-washed dishes and utensils lay. She filled a glass with water and set all three items neatly in a row on the kitchen floor in front of Brian. She brought out what was left of a five-pound sack of Gold Medal flour from the lower cupboard and poured those last few ounces of rich white powder into the pan. "Ready to stir?" she asked.

Brian, eyes popping with delight, reached for the spoon. "Now, should I now?"

"You stir an' I'll add water. Stir easy."

Soon they had about two ounces of paste. "Can I eat some?" Brian asked.

"Just a little. We can each taste a little. It's better cooked up nice and brown."

Brian put a big spoonful in his mouth and his eyes rolled in delight as he murmured "eehmm goob."

"That's too much!" Susie took the spoon away and made a tiny morsel for herself. She rolled it around her tongue and loved its morphing into sweetness as saliva diluted and digested it. "It's good but wait till we cook it brown like Momma does."

Susie used the stepstool to put the sauce pan on one of the stove's electric burners and turned it on. "Go watch the TV. It's got to cook a minute," she said leading Brian by the hand back to the television. She snapped it on, intending to go back to cooking, but there was Santa Claus and Mrs. Claus and a whole bunch of elves around a dining room table laden with a turkey and mashed potatoes and pumpkin pie. These two Adirondack urchins were transfixed. "What they eatin'?" asked Brian.

"That's Santa's family. They havin' a Christmas dinner."

The elves were acting up, shooting peas at each other with spoons. Santa snuck a thumb-full of pumpkin pie. Mrs. Claus tried to get him to concentrate on carving the turkey.

Brian giggled. Both kids salivated and dreamed of such a meal of their own. "Do they have pizza for Christmas?" Brian pleaded. "I'd want some pepperonis on mine."

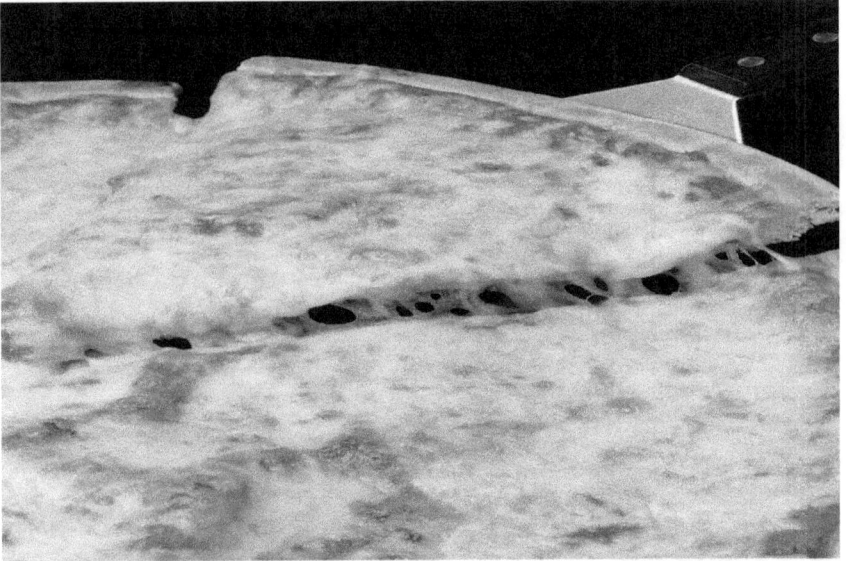

"I don't think they do but that'd be good. Look at that little elf with the peg leg. He's sneakin' some of that red stuff."

"Funny smell." Brian said, sniffing and looking around.

Susie sprang to her feet and ran into the kitchen. There, smoke poured from the pan on the stove. She ran screaming into her mother's bedroom. "Momma, the stove's on fire." She shook the unresponsive bundle buried in covers. "Momma, wake up; call the fire engine." She ran back into the kitchen, grabbed a broom and knocked the smoking pan onto the floor. There was nothing left of the bap but charred cinders.

Brian was screaming in terror. Susie rushed to the sink and got a glass of water that she threw on the still-smoking mess that hissed for a moment, and then stopped.

Susie pulled Brian to her, hushing him. "Shhh, quiet. It's OK. Fire's out."

Brian peeked out from the cover of his sister's sweater, took a breath and coughed on the smoke. Susie went to the bedroom door and closed it saying, "Guess Momma is real tired."

Footsteps pounded up the back way and the kitchen door burst open with Peter and then Mikey close behind. Their heads were out of their sweatshirt hoods now. Peter, the lanky six-footer with long blond hair and a wisp of a moustache, was in the lead. "What's going on? You tryin' to burn the house down? Where is your momma?" he shouted.

Mikey, his shaven head glistening like Mussolini's in the glare of the bare overhead light bulb, was the slower moving and shorter of the two. He surveyed the scene and calmly said, "Pizzz, fire's all out."

But Peter had taken hold of Susie's thin shoulders and was shaking her, "What's going on here? You want to get the cops here? You want to get us thrown out on our asses. It's cold out there. Where's your momma?"

Mikey stepped between them, quietly freeing Susie and facing Peter. "Cool it. Fire's out. Don't be wakin' up the neighbors."

Susie grabbed Brian and the two of them hid behind Mikey. Mikey turned to them saying, "You two OK? Nobody burned?"

Susie said, "We're OK, we was makin' bap but it got burned up."

"Bap?" Mikey said. "You mean with milk and flour in a pan and you try to make it brown on the bottom?"

"Uh, huh, but you can use water, too," nodded Susie.

"My ma used to make bap when we were out of food coupons. Jesus, it was good. I couldn't wait till we was out of coupons. Peter, you ever have bap?"

"No, I never had no bap and I don't even believe you ever had a mother."

"Well I did, till her old-fart boyfriend kick me out. I get a little bigger I'm going back and kick his ass out."

Susie's finger went to her lips "Shhh, you gotta be quiet. Momma sleepin'."

Brian sucked his thumb.

"Huh, we don't gotta' nothin'," Peter said. He opened the ancient refrigerator. "Nothin' in here. Light don't even go on." He slammed the refrigerator closed, then smirked, "Hey, you know what the mouse said when the old lady asked him what he was doin' in the fridge? He said 'This is a Westinghouse, isn't it? I'm just 'westing.' Get it. He was 'westing.' Ha ha."

Susie put her shushing finger to her lips, "Shhh, be quiet, Momma's in there sleepin'," and she pointed to the bedroom. Peter raised his shoulders, put a finger to his own lips and did a mocking tiptoe toward the living room.

Brian giggled at the sight.

Mikey laughed gently. "We could open some windows but there ain't that much smoke and it's cold out there."

Peter called from the living room in a stage whisper, "Nice TV in here. We could get a couple of bucks for it at the Greek's. Where's the remote?"

"Don't have a remote," Susie answered.

Mikey moved to the living room door, "Greek won't take it without a remote. Let's get out of here."

Brian trailed behind Peter, "You wanna' watch the alligator show?"

"Might be a good show," Peter said lowering his lanky frame into a bean bag chair that was leaking plastic pellets. "Come on, sit on my lap, little tiger." And Brian started toward him.

But Mikey was right there. "None of that stuff," he said grabbing Peter's thin arm. With a yank, he had him on his feet and moving toward the kitchen. "Come on, numb nuts, I gotta eat. Let's go shake the Pizza Tree."

Brian ducked out of the way into Susie's arms and both of them echoed, "Pizza Tree?"

"You kids be good. Stay away from that stove. Let your momma do the cookin'," Mikey called as, in their Nike Air Zoom Vick Threes, the boys clumped through the kitchen and down the back stairs.

Susie and Brian pulled two bean bags together in front of the television and switched on "Krypto the Super Dog." They pulled an afghan around them that their mother had stolen from her parent's house when she first got pregnant and ran away.

Susie remembered the flour bag and went to the kitchen to bring it back. They tore it into pieces and got great pleasure licking off the remains of the flour. "Wish this was pizza," Brian said.

"Or turkey. I wonder if there is a turkey tree, too," his sister said as Krypto, the big hero dog, rescued his little black partner from ferocious "Pit-bully."

Downstairs Mikey had a cell phone in his right hand while he inhaled deeply on a cigarette. He had found the cell during a previous shaking of the Pizza Tree. It was in a dumpster alongside the pineapple and salami pizza they had ordered. The phone reminded him of that delicious treat and his mouth watered. He could virtually taste the exotic mix of flavors. He and Peter had fed themselves with that trick all across the Adirondacks. They'd think of a weird pizza, order it over the phone, to be eaten in. When no one showed up and the proprietor despaired of selling it, he would throw it in the dumpster and the boys would dive in after. Trouble is, it can take all day to get served, Mikey thought.

Peter looked at him irritably. "Smokin'll kill yah. Yah know that?"

"Yeah, so'll not eatin'. What should I order?"

"We ain't got no dough."

"So we'll dig it out of the dumpster."

"I'm tired of that. That hamburger, cheddar cheese and sardines you dreamed up made me sick. Let's bop some delivery guy. We'll get some regular food and it will be hot." Then he added, "Maybe he'll be carrying some change, too."

Mikey thought for a moment, dragging in and then exhaling clouds of smoke into Peter's face and laughing as Peter frantically waved the fumes away. Mikey said, "You hurt another pizza guy and we'll be doin' jail time. You almost killed that last poor son-of-a-bitch with your ball bat."

"Cause you're too chicken to bop one."

"Don't make me bop you."

"You try it some time."

"Peter, all you need to do is scare the guy. He drops the food and runs. That's what they tell 'em to do. That's what I done when I was working for Papa John's. Don't make no sense to fight for a couple bucks."

"Just do it. Call that new place uptown, you been talkin' about. They won't be so careful."

Mikey pulled a flyer from his back pocket and laid it on the table, "Let's think about this a minute."

"Give me the damn phone, I'm hungry." With this Peter grabbed the phone and dialed the prominently displayed number.

"But where we gonna' nail him?"

"OK, OK, I'll handle it. I'll tell them it's a ski party. Free beer and big crowd comin'. Need a lot of food." Peter dialed the number from the slinger.

When Peter hung up Mikey was all over him. "You stupid jerk; 15 Millicent is just down the street from us. We'll get caught sure."

"It's home delivery, ain't it? Why should we walk? It's an empty shack. And no one knows we live here. It's supposed to be vacant."

"You moron."

"Mikey, you worry too much. It's Christmas. The cops are all home eatin' turkey."

The boys moved into their position in the dark behind the vacant shack, Mike with great reluctance.

Brian had fallen asleep under the afghan. Susie slipped back over to her window and gazed listlessly out. Then a car bearing a triangular sign on its roof, "Fat Sam's," pulled to a stop and flashed a spotlight. Susie's eyes riveted.

Mikey had made the pizza call and he and Peter hid themselves in the darkness of an alley a few doors down. Lights from neighboring windows tempered the snowy gloom. Mikey walked out of the yard and in a friendly voice called. "Got some pizza for the party? Bring it around here."

A figure dressed in a bright red Santa suit and sporting a white beard popped out of the car and extracted two boxes and three bags. "Two pepperoni, large wings and four subs comin' up."

Pizza Santa started down the alley with his load when Peter charged at him waving his baseball bat, yelling "Run you sucker."

Susie leapt to her feet and exclaimed, "Look out!"

With a push of the bat Peter knocked the boxes and packages sprawling from Santa's arms and Santa ran for his car.

Susie could not believe what she saw. Brian woke and started a lazy whimper as he came over beside her and tried to understand.

Peter was yelling again, "Wait a second, you. You got any money? Give it here," as he ran after his victim.

Santa, a small but quick man, reached into his car, pulled out a pellet gun that was modeled after a military rifle but was a size too small to be convincing.

Mikey yelled, "Look out! Gun!"

Santa pumped the action and fired twice, hitting Peter once in the chest and once on the right cheek.

Peter hesitated, wiped blood from his cheek, and enraged, resumed his charge. He swung the bat and connected twice with Santa's head. The blows produced sounds like melons hitting a brick floor. The man fell into the snow. His red hat gone, a crimson halo formed in the snow around his head.

Susie gasped. "They killed Santa. He was bringing pizza for Christmas!"

Brian said, "There's pizza all over?"

Peter raised his bat to swing again at the still body but Mikey hung on to his arm. "Get the stuff. I think you killed him."

"What about money?

"Forget it, someone's out on the porch next door."

The boys scooped up the boxes and bags of food. They ran through the snow into their own temporary quarters downstairs from the children and disappeared.

Inside the boys threw the food on the kitchen table and themselves, breathless, into rickety kitchen chairs.

"I told you, just scare him," Mikey said.

"The prick had a gun."

"It was a toy."

"Yeah, look he shot me in the face," said Peter pushing his face into Mikey's and pointing at the quarter-inch bruise and the trickle of blood on his right cheek. "What if he hit me in the eye?"

"Come on, let's eat. This stuff is getting cold. Put some in the oven." Peter obediently turned the oven on low, put a bag of wings, a pizza and two subs into it and closed the door. Then they were transfixed by the wail of a siren and then two more. In the street outside there was a tumult as State Police and neighbors followed the tracks in the new snow into the house and poured in on them.

Upstairs, Brian and Susie heard the sirens and watched an ambulance streak by, then two State Police cars with their red and white bubble gum machines casting beams of jarring red and white light to pierce the dark. The kids watched the show in excitement and then fear as the posse of police and neighbors invaded the house.

There were shouted voices and noisy footsteps downstairs as the boys were arrested, handcuffed and taken away. Then all was silent again except for Tom and Jerry on television. Brian and Susie looked at each other. This time Susie was at a loss. Finally Brian said, "Does Santa have a Pizza Tree?"

"Maybe," she answered. "Let's look downstairs."

"Should we tell Momma?"

"She still sleepin'."

The two went silently down the dark back stairs and entered the first floor kitchen. The police had left the kitchen lights on but the place was deserted. They had taken along the food that remained on the table possibly for evidence.

The aroma of oregano, tomatoes and pepperoni still filled the kitchen and a little smoke came from the oven. Susie rushed to the stove and opened the oven door. She took a flowered hand towel from the cupboard and pulled the hot containers from the oven, spilling wings and subs and pizza in a cornucopia across the floor.

"It must have been a big Pizza Tree," Brian crowed.

Susie said, "I guess so."

"Can we have some?"

"We shouldn't waste it."

The children sat on the kitchen floor for their Christmas dinner and gorged on chicken wings, turkey subs and pepperoni pizza. Susie said, "Save some for Momma. She'll be hungry when she wakes up."

Back upstairs, Susie turned off the light that had flooded from their window and tucked the two of them into bed. Outside the snow had stopped and a bright moon shone on the deep snowy blanket that comforted their venerable home.

SARANAC SCREAM

Concealed way back in the Adirondack woods on an obscure road off Route 86 are two penitentiaries, the Ray Brook Federal Correctional Institute and the New York State Adirondack Correctional Facility. The uninformed public, when headed west away from the glitzy streets of Lake Placid and the wooded slopes of the High Peaks, pass within a half mile of them. Just before the traveler's bulging SUV's and dusty sedans plunge into the solid resort town of Saranac Lake, they pass Old Ray Brook Road at State Police Headquarters.

The curious and the penitent who travel down that road will find new, low-lying, brick Federal buildings tucked among the evergreens but the State Facility is a creaking, gaunt giant of a Tuberculosis Sanitarium done over with coils of razor wire to storehouse medium- security State offenders.

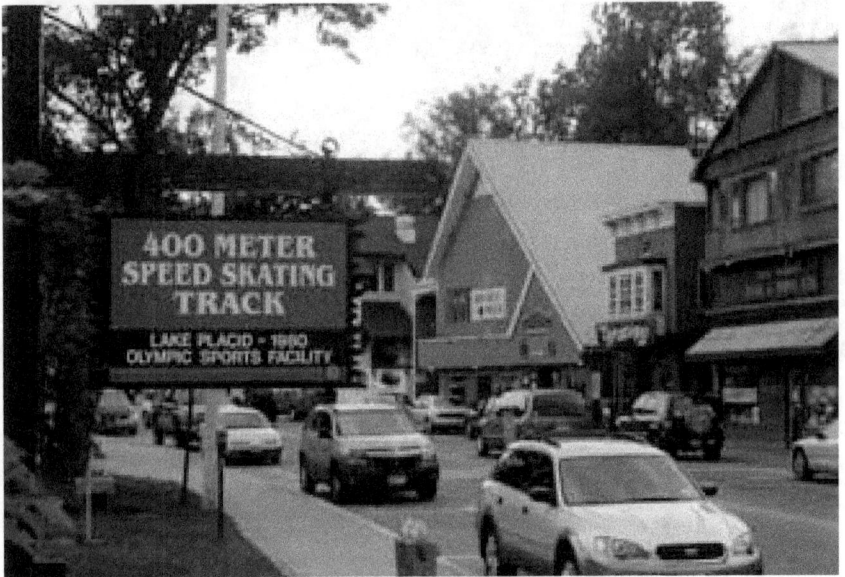

Once, in search of cheap down for insulating sleeping bags, the proprietor of The Mountaineer, the outdoor equipment shop in Keene Valley, tried to persuade the wardens of these two institutions to raise geese on a large scale. This would occupy the prisoners, feed them and provide a cash crop. The wardens told him that a steady diet of goose would not go down well with prisoners and therefore rejected his suggestion.

Now, deep in the basements of the old has–been hospital, we find a naked, shivering, filthy man mumbling. This naked hungry man has had nothing like the warming comfort of goose down or roast goose for some time. Listen to him.

Saranac Lake Town Hall

My name is Ali. I must hold on to my name. There are people who love me and care what happens to this wreckage that was my body. I am Ali, Ali, Ali. I haven't told them that, yet.

Once I was in line to lead the Nebuchednezar Division, pride of the Republican Guard. My little mother's pride as first in the study of the Quran at Sheik Abdel Kader Mosque. My father's delight when I received highest honors in Political Science at Baghdad University. We students would revolutionize the Near East, restore the glory of our ancient Mesopotamia, renew it with science and technology. Saddam and the Baath party showed the way. The way was ruthless and terrible but it was the only way.

If I'd been born here like my cousin Habib, I'd have been an Eagle Boy Scout, gotten a Harvard degree and be either a Senator or CEO of a Fortune Five Hundred Company. Anyway, that's what my blessed little mother says.

These bastards don't know any of that. They don't know that I ran the Baghdad Inquisition. They will get that out of me, too, and everything else. But I will make them work for it. By Allah, by my father and by the blood of all my dead brothers, these sniveling jackals will have to work for it.

Until... well, every man breaks. I know. I've seen it. I've broken the toughest, the hard cases. I've seen them brazen, they think their balls are made of brass. They spit in your face, ready for anything, just like me. And I have seen the life drain out of their rheumy eyes and watched them moulder into quivering heaps of shit that will tell you anything, anything at all to make it stop. Yet I defy these pigs.

My papers are perfect. My trunkload of Rolex look-alikes are illegal but that's an offense they look the other way on all the time. I flew into Montreal, bought an old Jeep Cherokee and drove over the Ivy Lea bridge. With my perfect English I should have passed. But this semitic nose and Meditereanean complexion or some nervous twitch I don't know about set off an alarm in that Immigration Officer.

It's cold here. I have had no clothes since I've been in this stinking hole. The worst of the stink is me. The odor would be worse but in this January cold, smells are stifled. For a little heat, I would tolerate the stench of a thousand leprous pigs . This cold, the night cold, envelops you, clings to you, works its way down inside so that everything aches and aches. I pray for numbness to let me sleep but sleep does not come. Yes, godless, Sunni dog that I am, even I pray now.

These jackal-sons-of-whores, are good. They would have done well in my intelligence unit, "the Baghdad Inquisition." I worked for Saddam himself. Those were good days. Don't think about them. Don't think about Chivas Regal, blonde show girls and Mercedes cars. We owned Baghdad and turned it into Babylon , no, Las Vegas. What a hell of a show. Who thought I would fall so far as to work for Al Qaida. Those sophomoric puppies. We would squeeze them to entertain Saddam, till they ran purple, like plump grapes.

Don't think that now.

My first trip upstairs for that CIA prick's interview, I still had my clothes. They put the sack over my head, cuffed my hands behind my back and helped me through the door with a kidney kick. It left me with a pain whenever I try a deep breath.

New York State Adirondack Correctional Facility
Razor Wire

I was tough then. In the interrogation room I spit in the CIA prick's face. I saw him smile and then the guard hit me in the back of the head with that big Colt 45. I was out and then dazed . I came around with the damn bag over my head again, suffocating me. The CIA was saying, "We need your help. We need all the help we can get to stop this war that is busting up your country. Believe me, we'd like to do this some easy way but whatever it takes we will do it." He said this quietly in that jocular friendly way John Wayne does in war movies, chastising some young Marine. "I'll see you again," he said and I imagined the Duke's wink and nod.

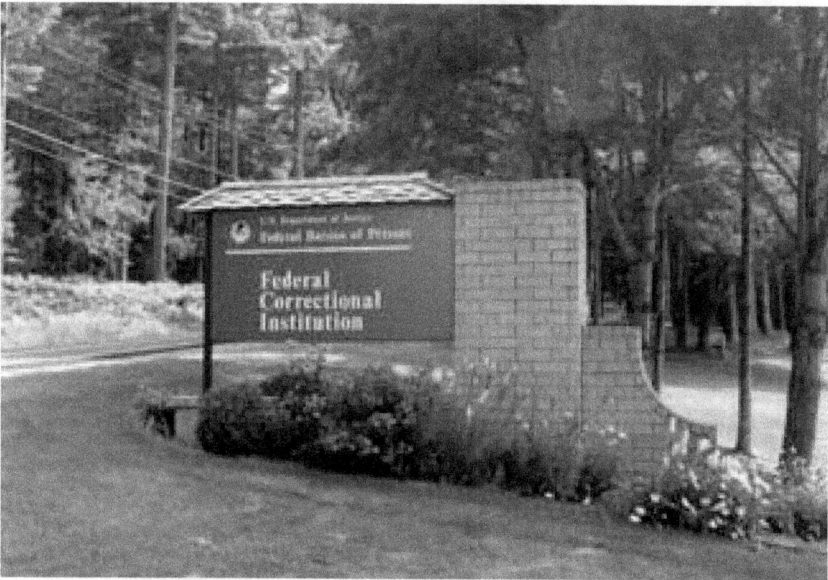

I told him in Farsi, "Your mother sells herself to garbage pickers and you are a queer, a mongol piece of dog shit. Go make love to yourself." I swore that next time I'd put that in English for him. They shoved me out of the room, down a hall. I heard someone screaming. Then they let me trip and fall downstairs . They picked me up and threw me back in my hole. In there, two of them grabbed me by the arms and threw me up against the rough stone wall three times. I fell to the floor. I couldn't breathe through my nose. I gasped for breath swallowing salty liquid, blood. The bag over my head was soaked with it. They left the hood and handcuffs on for something like 24 hours.

I don't really know how long I've been here, maybe three weeks. Food doesn't come on a schedule. No outdoor light comes in here so I can't tell day from night. In this cell, one bright lightbulb shines continuously, sealed behind a plexiglass plate. The only night comes when they put on the hood and cuffs.

Every few days they have broken   up this blur of undivided time with a trip upstairs. They took my clothes away the first day. I had a bucket for a toilet. They took that. Food came maybe once a day or every other day, always the same, rice and turnips. And there were cockroaches. I tried to kill them but they kept coming back. I studied them, watched where they hid, how they moved, counted their legs. They were my distraction, my television.

I played old movies in my head like Kirk Douglas in *Paths of Glory* . These three French prisoners, they were really heroes but because they did not sacrifice themselves to German machine guns they were condemned by a French court martial to die. One prisoner picked up a cockroach and said, "This roach will live tomorrow and we will be dead." Another prisoner squashed the bug.

I will be like that dead bug. Let the roaches live, I thought.

The screams were hard to bear. Shrill sometimes, sometimes shrieks and groans and then silence. I wondered, these Americans claim they don't do such things. Could the screams be fake? Are they bluffing?

A litany ran through my head bastinado, boiling, the boot, brazen bull, water torture, denailing, flagellation, flaying, foot roasting, rape, pressing, pitch capping. My own technicians used to read that list to our detainees and tell them these were simple Christian techniques taken from the time when the Catholic Church was forced to employ such methods to preserve the faith.

Adirondack Correctional Facility

Even then there were times that I would think, why
was all this cruelty necessary. I mean who really likes these
things, this cruelty, this terror and ugliness. It can only be the
perverted ones, sadists. Then there are those of us forced by
necessity into the business, this dirty business. The modern
world recognizes that torture is necessary and yet virtually
every nation in the world has signed treaties foreswearing such
beastiality and everyone uses it.

Saddam would say "Ali, you are such a humanitarian
but hypocrisy serves our national necessity. Be as gentle as you
like. See that they tell us what they know."

As long as each nation insists that captives must die
honorably without telling their secrets, we must hurt them.We
can't believe them even when blood starts running in bubbles
from their begging mouths. We know they will try to die
honorably and we know how wasteful is their effort for they
will tell us what we want to know. It is a simple fact, everyone
breaks.

Today when they came for me, I asked again for a
blanket. The sergeant said "Sure, old buddy. Got to have you
decent." Then this nice fellow brought in a bucket and covered
me with ice cold water before his two uglies dragged me up to
the CIA prick.

That CIA got up out of his fancy swivel chair as if
surprised and said , "Hey, what is this? This guy is soaking
wet. He's freezing to death." He said it so he made me believe
he gave a shit. The bastard, may a thousand devils feast on his
roasted balls in deepest hell. I know just how he did that. I
have played that game, too. Now comes a little comfort from
him before he tells them to turn up the pain. I must take what
strength I can from this.

"That's no way to treat him," the CIA in his khaki
jacket and Donald Duck Tee shirt said, swooping up and
handing me a wooly blanket, khaki-colored and with US in
black letters across it. He had taken the pains to warm it on a
chair by the wood stove that stood in front of his military desk.
He motioned me into the chair after I had wrapped my
nakedness in the lovely blanket. Then he poured strong black

tea from an iron kettle on the stove into a porcelain mug. He pushed the mug into my hands and motioned to a crystal bowl of sugar cubes on the stand by the chair.

A thousand calories a day in rice and turnips leaves you cold and hungry. I warmed my hands on that marvelous cup, breathed in the steam and sucked that godly nectar through sugar cube after sugar cube. A vision of my little mother pouring steaming tea in a mug and urging "Wear your new sweater. Take care of my favorite boy, my jewel," she'd say and muss my hair.

Placid Olympic Stadium

I cringed, waiting for the rabbit punch or the rope around my wrists to hoist me to the ceiling or whatever was next. But my shuddering calmed and I struggled not to believe in the illusory deliverance I knew he must offer. The tea and sugar coursed through me. I felt a glorious warmth blooming inside of me and a glint of wary optimism forced its way into my consciousness against my will and my judgement. This CIA John Wayne, he was doing his job like I did mine. We were both reasonable men. Perhaps I could barter some kind of an end to this with stories I could tell him and names. I could even offer him my utopian proposition that if no one had to keep secrets we could legalize this torture business of ours and never have to use it, or was I delirious?

"Ali, you look terrible," he said.

So he knows my name.

Lake Placid

"We don't know much about you. But you understand English so well and we have a photo that is your own spitting image. You had a chauffeur driving a big armored Mercedes for you when one of our guys messed it up with an RPG round. That makes me think you could be a high-value customer. What I don't get is how a high-ranking Saddam guy like you is running errands over here for Al Qaida. You're not supposed to be on the same side. Tell me about it."

It is my time. I am not so strong as I thought and not as stupid. I do not want my shoulders dislocated with the Palestinian hanging. I do not want these uglies to turn sour on me, open that stove door and roast my feet. The screams and all these wasted days are enough. My father was a practical man. He would say, "Ali, my son, be strong, do right, obey the Quran but be sensible."

"My good friend," I say over my tea. "Mr. CIA, there is much I can tell you and I will tell it to you. Your job was my job. I can help you. I know what will make our hot heads talk sooner. Myself, I will give you names, dates, places. Like they say, 'I know where the bodies are buried.' But I do, I really know where they are buried. I can show you the fabled WMD of your President's, so-called, imagination."

"Ali, you are wandering off the point already."

"I must have my clothes. You must feed me. You must treat me as the Geneva conventions say."

"Ali, my boy, we don't have to treat you any special way. Since you were in this business, you know that. But I do respect your offer of cooperation and I plan to take you up on it. But we need insurance. You need to feel some real pain to insure that you know this is serious business."

"What, what insurance? I will tell you everything."

"Yes you will," he said. And then, "Now if you are finished with that tea, boys, cuff this squealer."

The two uglies, one grabbed the cup. The other jerked me to my feet and yanked my hands up behind me. I could feel a searing pain as he clamped plastic cuffs onto my wrists. I was stunned, taken in by the oldest of routines. I had hoped, dreamed that I had a remnant of control. I have none.

"Hoist him up. Let's hear that squeal." My arms were forced up behind me. I fell sideways and saw overhead a rope suspended from an iron loop in the ceiling. Then a violent yank on that rope shot pain through my arms and shoulders. With a sickening crackle I swung by my wrists and contorted, upward into the middle of the room.

Now it was my screaming that terrified the others.

Do you here that screaming back in the forest? It comes from one of the wide verandahed rooms that used to offer coughing, cachetic victims of the White Plague, TB, a chance of recovery in sunshine and fresh air.

LAWMAN DOWN

There used to be a place in North Creek called Diamond Lil's. Behind the bar there one day, Lillian Folger breathed a cloud of moisture on to a glass and then polished it away with tender skill. Lil's graying hair, teased into a pile of blond curls, surrounded a cheerleader's face. In her late thirties, that face commanded a truly buxom bosom.

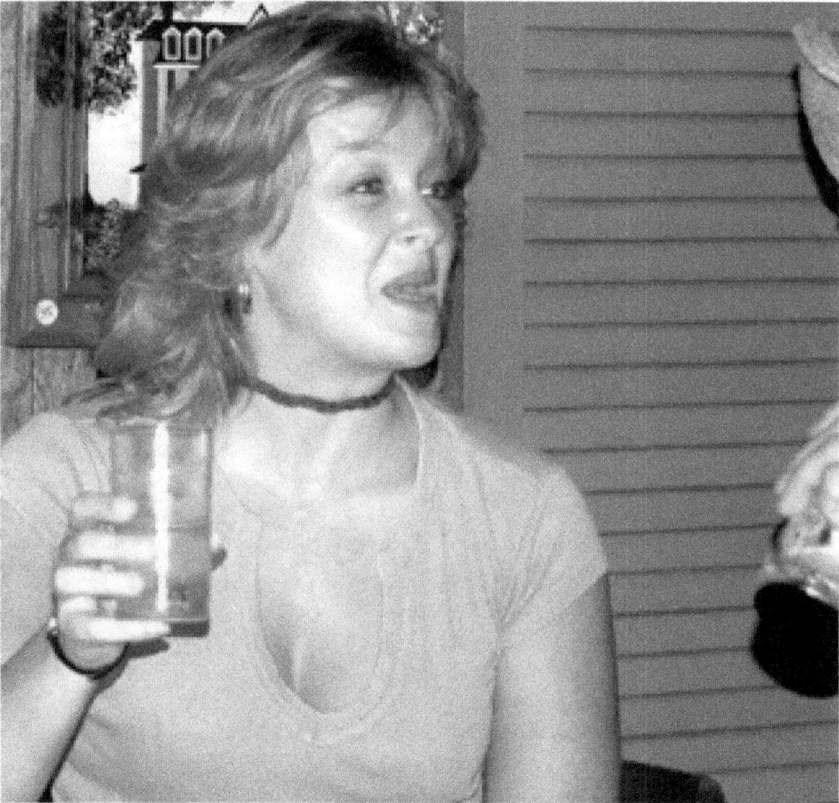

A full-length picture of her, lying naked in all her blond glory, hung on the wall opposite the bar. When a question of taste was raised, her husband, Sheriff Hank Folger, would respond, "Hell yes, when you got it, flaunt it."

Eben Saunders leaned his paunch into the bar and ran a chubby finger under Lil's chin. "How's my girl? You got time for a rich old man anymore?"

"Cost you five dollars," she said with a lascivious wink.

Eben reached for his wallet, licked a thumb, pulled out a ten dollar bill, laid it on the counter saying, "I'll take two."

It was early afternoon and on that blustery day there was little business stirring in town and only this in Diamond Lil's. "Put your money away. You know, Mister Johnsburg Town Supervisor, since you got elected, your money's no good here." She leaned over and gave him an affectionate kiss on the mouth. She and Hank, had mortgaged to the hilt to have this bar installed in North Creek's ancient Weller House. Eben held the mortgage.

Eben was slipping a hand down Lil's shoulder toward a breast when the tall uniformed figure of Deputy Sheriff Patrick Kirby appeared among the reflections of bottles in the great mirror behind the bar. Close after Patrick was Pop

Cassidy, one-eyed mountain guide and part-time bartender. Pop was in a plaid woolen shirt and heavy back-country trousers. He stamped his boots and slapped his woolen cap on his thigh to shake off snow. "Winter's comin'," he announced.

Patrick said, "Where you been, Pop? Winter's here a week already." But Patrick's thoughts were on Eben. What's that turkey up to? Is he trying to beat my time with Lil? He had heard talk of something going on between them, when he first got to town a year before.

Patrick had met Lil's husband, Sheriff Hank Folger, at a week's ordinance-training session in Albany. They quickly became friends. When the Town decided it needed another deputy, Patrick came to Hank's mind and he hired him. Patrick never imagined it was in himself to double-cross a friend and a boss, but it was.

Eben cleared his throat and leaned away from Lil winking, "Congratulations Lil, this is the second month in a row you've made your mortgage payment on time." He picked up his money and stuffed it back in his wallet, laughing.

He turned to Patrick, "Good afternoon, Deputy. Get your ration of speeders on good old Route 28 today? Got to keep the Town funded you know. That's your duty." He tapped an index finger on Patrick's chest.

Patrick elbowed Eben aside and took his place in front of Lil, saying, "Eben, don't you have to go review your militia or something?"

"Don't be making fun of the North Creek Minutemen, Deputy Kirby. More than once those boys have saved a sheriff's ass around here. Pop, tell this youngster about the time those timber thieves killed Sheriff Ned Wiggins. This boy's new in town; got to learn our ways."

Pop leaned his elbows on the bar, the eyebrow above his missing left eye arched reflexly and he began, "The way I heard, it was back in 1904. Ned was a real good sheriff, well-liked by all. He went out to confront this jobber and his gang about some illegal timber harvestin' and..."

"Yeah, yeah, it's a wild story." Patrick took over and told the account in one long breath. "Jobber bushwhacked the Sheriff, at least that's the way it looked. Those militia boys got into some liquor, burned down the jobber's camp and hung him along with three of his boys. Two of them boys weren't sixteen yet. Hung 'em off the Railroad Bridge. Never had an investigation, asked a judge or nothing. Whole idea scares the livin' shit out of me."

Lil stepped into the exchange, "Patrick, Honey, I was holding off having lunch till you got here. You're late," she smiled.

"Salesman going through here. Trying to do his books while he was driving. Skidded off the road. Pop and me towed him out of the ditch."

"Was he hurt?" she asked.

"No. Banged his nose. There was a lot of blood but he's OK. I sent him along with a warning."

"Should have give' him a ticket," Eben said. "Next time he'll run into you or me. Kill someone."

"So how about a plate of spaghetti and meatballs," Lil offered. "In commemoration of all the blood. Cook just made up nice new red sauce."

Pop said, "I'm all set. I'll watch the bar if you all want to go eat." Looking at Lil and pointing out the door, he added hesitantly, "Cupid's in the pickup..."

"Bring her in. She's the only trained corpse-smelling dog I ever heard of. She gives the place some color." Lil laughed and took Patrick by the hand into the dining room.

Eben got up, put on his Stetson and said, "If you're bringing that dog, Stupid, in here, I'm going. She stinks."

Pop said, "Her name's Cupid and you smell a lots worse to her than the other way around. She's trained at smellin' out corpses."

"Spaghetti, Eben?" Lil offered again.

"No thanks. I've got to go to see if the electric is installed into that chalet they're putting up for me. Going to be a beauty. I'll sell it for a fortune." He started for the door.

"Come back soon Mister Supervisor," Lil threw after him with that wink of hers.

After a hearty lunch and a glass of Chianti, Lil and Patrick wound up in bed in the owner's apartment on the hotel's second floor. They had been seeing each other like this for six months. Hank was a popular, busy guy. He was head of the Gore Mountain Ski School and a member of the Town Planning Board. Wherever he went, he put himself in charge. But he left Lil to her own devices. Patrick, a recent widower from out of town, was fair game.

Patrick had spells of guilt over this quick betrayal of his new boss but Lil made it all seem natural. He once asked her, in post-coital remorse, "Don't you think this is wrong? Isn't it a sin?"

Caressing him, she responded, "Oh, I don't think God writes these things down in His little book."

Patrick was pulling on his pants and Lil still lolling in bed. The police radio in the sitting room blared, "All points alert, all points alert, for a late-model, white pickup occupied by a Caucasian couple. They are believed to be perpetrators of armed holdups across New York State.   MO: Woman,

complaining of pain, distracts attendant. Male companion
disables attendant, before an alarm can be sounded."

The voice broke off its formal tone and went on, "This is for Hank Folger. This is Sheriff Pete Thompson in Indian Lake. Clerk down at the Lake Store got a pretty good description of a couple in a vehicle that sounds like the one we're looking for. They're headed down Route 28 toward you in North Creek. We need you and Kirby to get out to that squeeze in the road by the cemetery and set up a road block. Be careful, this pair is armed and dangerous. He's a two-time loser and she's a junky."

Hank Folger's commanding voice broke in, "Reading you loud and clear, Pete. I'm at the Landing Strip; I'll be by the squeeze in five."

Lil picked up the mike and keyed it, "Hank, I'll locate Patrick and tell him to meet up with you at the diner. You can go out together. No sense gettin' anyone killed."

The radio crackled as Hank keyed the other end. "No time to waste. Get Patrick out to the cemetery as quick as you can. I'm on my way. Over and out."

"Stupid bastard," Lil spluttered. "He'll get his self killed."

Patrick thought, Hank, that fucking cowboy, wants to pull this thing off himself and he could easy get us both killed. Well, let him.

Snow was falling; the road was slick. Patrick did not proceed with all haste. He did not turn on the siren or the bubble gum machine on top of his cruiser and he did observe the town speed limits.

A few miles away, Mike Shaughnessy and Winona Kurtz sped down Highway 28, windshield wipers beating rapidly to keep the windshield clear of falling snow. Mike huddled over the steering wheel. He was a big, good-looking guy in his late thirties. He had on a Texas straw hat that he wore summer and winter and about a five-day beard. Winona was husky and pretty and wore a perpetual smile that had lately turned to pleading sadness. The change made Mike love her more and more and swear never again to desert her; never to surrender himself to "the man" again and go back to confinement.

"All I got left are these Percodan and that bottle of Tylenol," Winona showed him a small handful of capsules. "And my back aches so bad."

"I know, I know Honey, but that guy back in Indian Lake looked like he made us."

"But I hurt so bad with all this driving. Can't we get out and walk. Get something to eat."

"There must be an All Points out on us. We got to keep moving. Find a place to hole up."

"You'll get us out of this, I know, but I just got to stand up and walk. Sitting kills my back. Pain's going down my legs."

"Hold on, Baby. We'll find another one of those swanky ski chalets with nobody home, a medicine cabinet full of Darvon and a kitchen full of whiskey and steak."

She smiled up at his handsome face and ran a small hand along his thigh. "That place at Placid was a real honeymoon for us. I'm so tired of this running, why can't they leave us alone, forget about us?"

"The sons-of-bitches just don't want to give up. They don't understand when enough is enough. Don't you worry, Honey. We'll get by. And there's always this." He patted the 38 Smith and Wesson revolver tucked against his belly, to the right of the silver rodeo belt buckle he had won in McAlister.

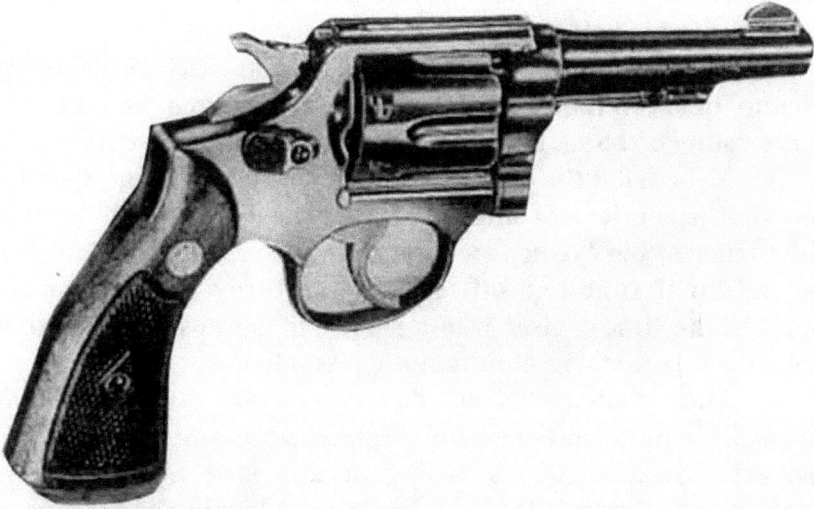

Then he crooned to her:

"Oh, the buzzin' of the bees in the cigarette trees near the soda water fountain,

At the lemonade springs where the bluebird sings on the Big Rock Candy Mountain..."

Then through the falling snow a flashing red and white light appeared. An instant later the hulking outline of Sheriff Hank Folger's cruiser blocking the road was illuminated by the pickup's headlights. "Son-of-a-bitch," Mike screamed jamming on the brakes and skidding to a stop. The pickup's rear end slid around forward so the truck ended broadside to the road and stalled. Mike tried the ignition key furiously but the engine didn't catch. Then he made the sign of the cross as Sheriff Folger walked out of the gloom, heavy flashlight held high in one hand, the other resting on a holstered 38 Smith and Wesson of his own.

"God damn it," whispered Winona.

"Take it easy," said Mike gritting his teeth.

Mike opened the door part way with his left hand, right hand on the wheel, both in plain sight. "What's up, Officer? You gave us a scare."

He felt Winona's hand on his belly. He felt the metal barrel of the revolver trace a line on his skin as she slipped it from under his belt.

Hank lowered his flashlight. Mike kicked open the pickup door. Winona raised the pistol an inch and blasted three rounds, "bang, bang, bang," into the Sheriff's chest.

Mike tried the engine again. It roared as he jammed his foot on the accelerator and threw the wheel to the right. Out of the corner of his eye he saw a second cruiser slam to a halt just behind the first and an officer leap out, throw his body on the hood of the first cruiser into a steady firing position and then open up with a storm of automatic pistol fire.

Mike yelled, "Keep down," as he shoved Winona toward the floor. She winced in agony as the sudden flexure of her arthritic spine sent lightning streaks down both legs. Two rounds sang through the cab. He ducked low to the far side of the wheel and listened to the rear tires explode in succession. With the door banging on each swerve the pickup careened away into the dark. Mike prayed to the Virgin, "Holy Mary Mother of Christ, don't let them hit the gas tank."

A couple miles back up 28, at a curve, they went into a long skid. Mike turned into it and then away and back into it. He saw it in slow motion as they inexorably floated through slush and into a ditch with the center of the pickup's body hung up on a boulder. They sat in the tilting cab for a moment, hearts slowly giving up their pounding. They embraced and Winona sobbed.

Mike said, "Thank you, God. Thank you." Then to Winona, "They won't be after us soon. That Sheriff is going to want to take care of his buddy, even if he looks dead."

"Is he dead? asked Winona. "If he's dead, we're fucked for sure."

"They haven't caught us yet. We're close to the Canadian border. The Good Lord willing we'll get across."

"But we killed someone. We killed a fucking cop."

"He didn't give us a choice."

"What are we going to do?"

"It'll be hours before they get another car here. They won't get a search party going at least til' tomorrow."

Winona interrupted, "The truck's no God damn good. We are fucked can't you see."

"But we've got our gear. We could camp out for a week. And see if the Lord doesn't lend us one of those rich folks' ski palaces. Maybe with a Jeep Grand Cherokee in the garage. Got to have faith, Honey."

They climbed out of the truck, pulled on hats and zipped parkas. Mike unloaded backpacks from the bed of the pickup.

Winona stretched saying, "Jesus, my back feels better standing up. I'd rather walk out of here than ride another mile."

"We can't walk out of here over these mountains. We'd need snowshoes up higher."

The pair put on the backpacks and took off up the road looking for side roads to developments. Mike turned to walk backwards a few steps and said, "Look, snow's covering our tracks already. They won't know which way we went or if we hitched a ride out of here."

Winona said, "I shouldn't have done it. I shouldn't have shot that son-of-a-bitch. We are truly fucked." "Don't talk like that, Honey.   We'll hide long enough to steal a 4X4 and make run for Canada. Say a Hail Mary with me. Ask her to help us. Hail Mary Full of Grace..."

Patrick had emptied his service revolver's six rounds at the truck disappearing up the road into a snowy haze. He quickly ejected the empty shells and reloaded in place without standing upright. Then he backed away from cover of the cruiser aware that the truck might come back for a try at running around the road block now that one officer was down.

Hank was lying still in the road flat on his back where he landed. Patrick reached into the cruiser, keyed the microphone and yelled, "Lawman Down, Lawman Down. Ambulance and back up to the North Creek Cemetery, Route 28. Now! Right Now! God Damn it! There is a Lawman Down."

Glancing repeatedly up the road for any indication of returning headlights, Patrick moved cautiously to where Hank sprawled on the snowy wet macadam in a widening pool of his own dark blood. The thought kept ripping through Patrick's head, if I'd have been here two minutes sooner. If I'd've been here two minutes sooner. Despite his caution he slipped to his knees and skidded in the blood so that he bumped into Hank's still body. Hank did not respond. Patrick felt for a carotid pulse and found none. He held a hand over Hank's open mouth and felt no movement of air.

Automatically he started CPR. He slammed Hank hard in the chest to start his heart. On his knees, he leaned over Hank and covered Hanks's lips with his open mouth. Sealing Hank's nose with one hand and forcing his head back into an arched position; with the other he gave two hard puffs. Bloody air bubbled from the chest wounds. Patrick moved to cover one hand with the other, found the xiphoid process measured two fingers up and leaned forcibly into the puddling ooze on Hank's chest. His thoughts raced on as he counted, 1,2,3, Fifteen times a minute, I think it's fifteen times a minute. 4, 5, 6, Oh Christ, I'm pumping the blood out of him. Bleeding, shit you're supposed to stop the bleeding first. 7, 8, 9. Where the hell could I put a tourniquet? Damn it. 10, 11, 12, I killed him. I should have been here. 13, 14, 15, And I was fucking his fucking God damn wife.

It was a fifteen minutes before the Johnsburg Emergency Squad arrived. They found the two officers in this grotesque embrace with Patrick, now, as bloody as Hank. One of the rescue workers took over CPR as Patrick stood up and then staggered to a seat in the snow.

A second rescue worker searched for Hank's pulse, shook his head, then shined a flashlight into Hank's fixed, dilated pupils and said, "He's gone. You can stop."

When Patrick got back to town, Eben was at the hotel. He had one arm around Lil comforting her and with the other he was dialing a phone to roust out the North Creek Minutemen. Patrick saw it all in a kind of haze. He had thrown a jacket on over his bloody shirt but his face and hands were smeared with drying blood. He embraced Lil' saying, "I was too late. I'm so sorry."

Lil recognized how shaken Patrick was. "You would have nailed those butchers if anyone could have. Hank would have appreciated what you done."

"Lil, I don't know what to say."

"Eben has got his Minutemen on it. They've got dogs and ATV's. They'll get 'em."

Pop Cassidy came out from behind the bar. "Patrick, you look terrible. Come over her to the sink. Let me wash some of that blood off you." He pulled a fresh towel out of a cabinet under the bar, soaked it in warm water and handed it to Patrick. Patrick stared at himself in the giant bar mirror, dabbing at his face with the towel, the reflection of Lil's nude painting haunting him.

"Hold on a second. I got a clean shirt in the back." Pop returned with a blue denim shirt. His dog, Cupid, had come over to circle Patrick excitedly, sniffing and whimpering. Pop tossed her an oyster cracker from a bowl on the bar. She snatched it in mid-air and gobbled contentedly. "Smells the blood. She took to that corpse hunting course real well," Pop said raising the eyebrow over his empty socket and shrugging.

Patrick gave Cupid a pat on the head, took the shirt and went into the washroom. "Let me get some of this off of me." He looked at the blood on his hands.

That night Eben and forty of his Minutemen volunteers set up road blocks, sent out armed search parties on foot, in ATVs and in 4x4's. Some of them searched well into the early morning hours of the next day but Eben and the party he had lead were home in bed by midnight.

Patrick was up all night on the phone. He received assurances of massive police support to track down the killers of such a popular and well-respected Lawman as Hank Folger. He set up an emergency operations center in the main parlor of the Weller House. He and volunteers hung maps on walls, set up radio equipment, broke out guns and ammunition.

During the early evening someone called in from Gore Mountain Ski Lodge to report hearing gunfire. One of the Minutemen told the caller that it was standard procedure for searchers to fire their weapons to insure that they were functioning and to keep track of where other search teams were. As Police, State Troopers and neighboring Sheriffs poured into North Creek, Patrick began working out the logistics of where they would stay and be fed.

At **8 am** the day after the murder Eben walked in smiling and looking surprisingly rested to Patrick. Patrick was behind a folding table made into an impromptu desk. A half-empty mug of coffee was at his elbow. There was a phone, a jumble of maps and papers in front of him. He was bleary with fatigue. Uniformed officers in grim, subdued conversations crowded the room.

Eben wore a signal orange neckerchief, the uniform of the Minutemen, and had a brace of Colt 45 pistols strapped around his heavy waist. He waved to the crowd. Several called him by name and waved as he walked through the room shaking hands. Lil came up to him and gave him a welcoming embrace. Eben hugged her saying, "Don't you worry, Honey, this is all being taken care of: They won't get out of the valley. Then he turned to the crowd saying, "First thing I want to do is post my personal $5,000 reward for the capture or the corpses of these criminals." A rumble of approval came from the crowd.

Then Eben pulled up a chair beside Patrick at the table. "So, where're we at here?" he growled.

Patrick thought, Eben looks awfully well-rested and fed for someone out searching the woods all night. So he said, "Where the hell you been? I had you and your dogs down for that section up in the woods alongside the ski hill."

Eben leaned forward and put a fist on the table, "I ask you again Deputy, how have you got things organized here? I see a bunch of useful men standing around scratchin' their asses."

Patrick stretched and yawned thinking, what's this nasty tone about? Then he answered wearily, "We're setting up a search headquarters here. I got Lil working out bunks. I'm just going over the maps to draw search quadrants."

Eben rolled his eyes, "You haven't sent any of these new guys out yet?"

"I got a team ready to go. We're going to start right here," and Patrick put a finger on the map near the new ski lift line.

"Christ, we just searched that last night! We can't disrupt the skiers. The season is just started."

"I want it gone over again, in daylight."

"That's damn nonsense. I was over that with my own team. You ever run a full-out search like this before?"

"I've done some search and rescue work and we are working out a plan here."

Eben stood up, slapped his hand to his head, "Working out a plan?" he exclaimed. "Deputy, the Minutemen have worked out a search and rescue plan over the last two years. You better let us handle this."

Is he trying to cover-up something or is he just trying to make me look bad? Patrick thought as the cobwebs cleared from his head with an adrenalin rush of anger. "I'm in charge here, Mister Supervisor. I am the Sheriff's department for North Creek and the Minutemen will do what I tell them to...or sit this one out."

Eben, standing and red-faced, turned to one of the Minutemen who had followed him in. All of them had donned their signal orange neckerchiefs. "Sy, write this down. You two men sign as witnesses," he pointed to two more.

Sy sat and took out a pen and pad. Eben dictated, "I, Eben Saunders, Supervisor of the Town of Johnsburg, do this second of December, 1965, formally suspend Patrick Kirby from all duties as a Deputy Sheriff in this town. Further I appoint myself temporary acting Sheriff until such time as a competent replacement for Sheriff Hank Folger can be found."

"Patrick, you're dismissed. Go home and get some sleep."

There was again a general rumble of ascent in the surrounding crowd. Lil came over and stood by Eben. Eben said to her, "Lil, those Lawman killers will not leave this valley alive." He took off his brilliant orange neckerchief and laid it possessively over her shoulders. Then they embraced.

Lil came away from Eben with tears in her eyes. She fondled the satiny material against her ruddy cheek and nodded coldly to Patrick, "Patrick go home. This will get taken care of without you."

The impact of what had just happened fell on Patrick like an avalanche. It numbed and engulfed him and carried him away. He dumbly picked up his hat and walked out of the hotel. I am the goat here. They are going to stick it to me. I should have got to that road block. What if the papers get hold of the story about me and Lil? A Lawman dead, shot in cold blood. Every Lawman will be focused on his own survival. They got to blame someone and they've got to draw blood. He felt those sentiments boiling in the grim crowd he was leaving.

No one said a word to him as he left.

For a week Acting Sheriff Eben Saunders orchestrated a search of the greater North Creek area, its mountains, forests, resorts and hundreds of part-time-occupied ski camps. No sign of the missing couple was found except for the truck disabled in a ditch. Nationwide alerts were sent out on the pair. The out-of-town police were starting to end their efforts. Eben didn't discourage them. He praised them for their "valiant and selfless efforts."

A week after the murder, the Village of North Creek organized a massive funeral for its beloved, now martyred, Sheriff Hank Folger. Police from all over the Adirondacks, and from upstate New York, Vermont and Canada, arrived to march in display of solemn solidarity in support of this fallen comrade.

Eben raised a fund and, with miraculous speed, arranged for the placement of an enormous red granite tombstone in the shape of two hearts intertwined to mark the dead sheriff's grave.

At the funeral service, there were speeches by politicians, police officials and old friends. Lil wore a black veil and was helped to the grave side by Eben. Ski tourists lined the streets gaping at the unforeseen spectacle. The Gore Mountain Ski Patrol and Ski School marched with the police. High School marching bands joined them from Lake Placid and Tupper Lake. North Creek's Prom Queen placed a bundle of dry winter field-gatherings at the foot of the monument and melted in tears as a lone piper began his wail.

Patrick spent the week brooding and drinking alone in the little camp he rented on the edge of town. He did not participate in the funeral except to watch at a distance from his pickup. The crowd dissipated after the interment. Patrick remained sitting and staring, wondering, what next? My sheriff career is in the toilet. What chief is going to hire a deputy who lets the boss get killed? Hank was a good guy and I let him down, more than one way. Lil and Eben seem to have buddied up. Is there going to be some kind of investigation for negligence? It could happen. Should I just pack-up and go. What the hell, might as well get drunk. He reached for a fresh pint in the glove compartment, wondering if anyone ever put gloves in there anymore.

Before he had the cap off the bottle, Pop Cassidy was knocking at the passenger's side window, his empty eye socket winking spasmodically. Patrick motioned him in.

Pop whistled Cupid into the back and climbed into the cab himself. He was shaking his head and holding out his left hand. "I need a slug of that." Patrick handed him the bottle he had opened and Pop took a long pull at it. Making a wry face, as the burning liquid shot into him he gulped, "I found 'em."

Patrick took the bottle back from him. Drank a soothing throat full and smiling at Pop said, "You found what?"

"I found the two stiffs."

"What two stiffs? Where?"

"I found the killers. Cupid sniffed 'em out. Up there behind Upper Stielhang Run."

"You been back on the sauce again, haven't you? You been dreaming, old man."

"This is my first shot in over a year. I needed it after seeing 'em up there all blue, heads half off. Coyotes been at 'em. Half ate one of their own, too."

"Better tell Eben, let him have all the glory for clearing this up."

"Thing is," Pop said rubbing his twitching left eyebrow. "That woods behind Upper Stielhang is where you sent Eben and his dogs that first night when he came back in early. Then he didn't want anyone to go there in daylight, like we done all the other night-searched areas."

"You think Eben found them that first night?"

"Looks that way to me."

Patrick started putting things together in his head but asked the question anyway. "Why didn't he report it ?"

"You tell me."

"Because him and his boys killed 'em?"

"Maybe."

"He really liked that story about the Minutemen and Ned Wiggins."

They drove out to the mountain and borrowed snowshoes and a snowmobile from an outfitter friend of Pop's. With Cupid bounding through the snow they followed an old woods road up the far side of the mountain deep into the high woods. There they parked the machine and strapped on snowshoes to hike a quarter of a mile through a dense, evergreen forest to a clearing made by a two hundred-year-old, blown-down hemlock whose uprooted base sheltered a patch of forest floor. Cupid ran ahead barking, whimpering and then circling near two dark, partially snow-covered objects.

"That's the two of 'em," Pop said nodding toward the lumps. He reached into his pocket to break off a piece of Milk-Bone to reward Cupid. She gobbled it, smiling her thanks with her whole body.

Patrick cocked his pocket-sized 35- millimeter Minolta and started snapping pictures from the sled. Then the two of them dismounted and approached the frozen corpses. Winona Kurtz was sitting upright, back against the roots. The 38 Smith and Wesson revolver was in her right hand, a bullet hole in her right temple, blue, frozen head inclined to the left. Exposed neck chewed into by something. Mike Shaughnessy lay just a few feet away, head split open as if that weapon had been fired into his skull repeatedly at close range.

Patrick took many pictures before he came close enough to nudge Shaughnessy's solid frozen torso with the toe of his boot. The corpse did not move easily. Frozen to the ground, Patrick thought.

Pop stayed close to Patrick. "Least they don't smell in this cold. Don't smell to us but Cupid's got a nose on her." Cupid was sniffing at the two back packs and some other gear strewn close by.

Patrick asked, "Did you touch anything?"

"No sir. I shot out of here like a bat from hell, soon as I saw what 'twas."

"We're the only ones that know they are here?"

"Far as I know. Less someone else wrote that note she's holding there." Pop pointed to a piece of cardboard the dead woman grasped in her left hand.

Patrick leaned close to her and read out loud, "We never meant to hurt anyone. Pain was so bad we had to steal medicine. Mike wouldn't hurt a flea. We decided to call it quits here. I had to shoot him. I shot the sheriff, too. Good Bye Ma, all my love. Winona Kurtz."

"Murder-suicide," said Pop.

"So it seems," Patrick answered but he had straightened up and was walking toward a moss-covered dead tree that had a gaping hole in its moss cloak. He took out a Swiss Army knife and dug into the punky hole till he found something hard. He held the silvery lump in the palm of his hand to show Pop.

Pop said, "45-caliber slug."

"Was somebody shooting at them?" Patrick asked the air.

The sound of approaching snowmobiles came through the woods. There were four or five of them. Patrick put his camera and the slug in a pocket. The snowmobile riders had not dismounted and snowshoed like Patrick and Pop. Instead, in their hurry, they crashed through the underbrush. They formed an arc blocking the route that Pop and Patrick had taken in. Orange neckerchiefs adorned their necks and Eben was at their lead.

Eben jumped from his sled into knee-deep snow and waded over to them. The four others held back and kept hands on holstered pistols. "Pop," he said, "we figured that you and Stupid were on to something. So you found 'em, huh?"

"Cupid's her name," Pop muttered.

"Well, you're up for the reward, anyway. Five thousand bucks."

Then he addressed Patrick, "Haven't seen you all week. What do you make of this?"

Patrick pursed his lips and shrugged, "Looks like they came up here, saw how hopeless it was. Then she shot him and herself. Usually it's the other way around."

"Well, he was probably a chicken-hearted son-of-a-bitch, shoot Hank the way he did," Eben said.

"OK boys, mystery solved. Load these poor dead sons-of-bitches on your sleds and get them out of here."

Patrick took a step away, put his arms out to halt the men saying, "Hold on. You can't do that. This is a crime scene. We need to get the lab out here to make sure we know what happened."

Eben yelled, "Nonsense, didn't you read the note. It's obvious what happened. You men get them out of here."

Patrick thought. When did he get to read that note? Then he stepped into the path of the nearest Minuteman, a slight young man, and gave him a shove. "God Damn it, Eben! This is a crime scene."

Eben unsnapped the holster of the Colt on his right hip and said in a loud even tone, "I'm the Sheriff. I have deputized these Minutemen. Patrick, if you interfere I'll have you taken into custody. Or I'll shoot you myself."

Patrick backed off. He and Pop watched the grisly sight as the two frozen corpses and their belongings were tied awkwardly to snowmobiles. If they weren't in such a hurry they'd go out for toboggans, Patrick thought, fingering the slug in his pocket and wondering what a crime lab could do with his pictures and that slug. We need autopsies to establish time of death and do ballistics on the slugs in their heads and anywhere else and check trajectories. I'd like a handwriting expert to tell me who wrote that note. I wonder if she has a "Ma."

He and Pop snowshoed back to their machine. Pop said, "Don't look right."

Patrick nodded.

" Damn vigilante Minutemen. Next you know they'll be going after out-of-season venison merchants. Think me and Cupid'll head back into the woods, till they get done providing justice."

"You don't want to help me put things straight?"

"Ain't no jury around here's going to pay attention to a prosecutor who wants to put their neighbors in jail for two sorry thieves they put out of their misery. It ain't right but that's the way it is."

"OK Old Buddy. I'll have to think on it. You go do what you got to do."

On returning to town Eben called a conference of town officials and persuaded them in the interest of the ski trade, the widow and the bereaved town folk that it would be best to ship the bodies and their belongings to Lake George for immediate disposal and cremation. The newspapers and various government offices were notified and the deed was accomplished forthwith.

Patrick drove over to Lake George the same day. He debated going to the Warren County District Attorney to obtain a court order and stop the destruction of evidence. But then he thought, what's it going to accomplish? The DA may not listen. Even if he does and we prove the Minutemen killed them, Pop is probably right, we couldn't get a conviction.

How to make something decent come out of this mess puzzled him. He left his film with a discreet photographer friend who promised them overnight. Next morning he put the photos and the 45-caliber slug in a safe-deposit box at the Evergreen Bank and he drove back to North Creek.

Eben and Lil were in the bar of the Weller House where Lil was holding court as town folk came by to offer condolences. Patrick came into the crowded room unnoticed. He made a sandwich at the buffet spread beneath Lil's nude painting and he bought a beer from the new college-kid bartender. He had nearly finished eating when he made eye

contact with Lil and she nudged Eben. Eben dressed formally in a western-cut suit that camouflaged his unhealthy waistline, looked up and walked over to Patrick.

Patrick didn't rise but he did look Eben in the eye. Eben said, "So, you want to talk?"

Patrick said, "OK."

"Come with me," Eben led the way into the room immediately behind the bar. Lil watching from across the room hurried to join them.

Lil said, "Good to see you, Patrick," but she stood by Eben with a hand looped inside his arm.

Eben said, "I understand you were in Lake George. You had us concerned you were going to stir up something but we have heard nothing. What's up?"

Patrick said, "I think you and your boys killed those two. Shot them in the head, execution style. Didn't give a God damn for the law."

Lil said, "They gunned Hank down while you were diddling around… somewhere."

Patrick said, "Yeah right, somewhere."

"Patrick," Eben said, "everyone that saw those two up there behind Stielhang, says that woman killed that man and then killed herself. She wrote a note, confessing."

"Eben, you made it look that way."

Eben stepped forward shaking his head in a conciliatory way, "Even if that nonsense were so, so what? We are well rid of those two scum and there is going to be no long, expensive trial."

Lil said, "Hank worked all his life for justice and justice has been served."

Patrick stood up and took Lil's hand, "I know how much Hank meant to you." He paused, smiling a puzzling smile. "I understand how you believe the score had to be made right. But I want it right, too."

Eben said, "What have you got in mind?"

"I've got your 45 slug out of a tree right alongside where they were executed. I have pictures of the crime scene and I have your haste in destroying the evidence."

Lil moved closer to Patrick, eyeing Eben accusingly. "You didn't tell it to me like that."

Eben said, "That's not much but what do you want for it?"

"I'll take the mortgage on this place and you can make me Sheriff."

Eben said "Done. You bring me those objects tomorrow morning and I'll have your badge and those papers."

"What about me?" Lil said.
Patrick looked at Eben, "You want to flip for her?"

LITTLE BITTY MURDERS

Charlotte wore blue jeans and a crimson angora sweater. For Al, the sweater set off her swirl of black hair like a nocturnal rifle blast. She laughed with mock outrage as he lifted her across one shoulder and hefted her into the front seat of his dusty Jeep Cherokee. Neither had actually murdered anyone before; not what a District Attorney would call a murder anyway.

Overhead, low Adirondack clouds threatened rain. Al had parked the ancient vehicle in a gravel drive alongside the cottage which Charlotte shared with her mother at the Forest Lake Motel on Route 73 outside Lake Placid. The complex was owned by a Pakistani family that had visa difficulty and hired Charlotte's mother as manager till they could enter the country. The place needed paint.

"Get the chicken. I made fried chicken for the potluck," Charlotte yelled. The tails of Al's red and black flannel shirt flapped outside his jeans as he swung his lanky frame around toward the driver's side.

The two made an odd contrast in physical types. Charlotte was compact and big-boned but strikingly beautiful in a dark voluptuous way. She had inherited her build from her father who had been a pro-wrestler. Al was a large, sinewy blond with long hair and a Fu Manchu moustache.

Al had cajoled Charlotte into this Saturday excursion despite her protests that she had to be back for another date by seven. She was an old girlfriend with whom he had not had a roll in the hay since he began law school the previous fall. His

Paul Smiths undergrad fraternity had planned a reunion picnic at the Adirondack Buffalo Company on the Blue Ridge Highway but only a few signed up. That morning Joe Milano, social chairman, called to cancel for rain.

Al had worried, should I tell her it's off? She might take advantage and wangle out of going.

He picked up the picnic basket from the cement stoop at the side door, then opened the back hatch of the Cherokee. "Hey, fried chicken, that's great. I'll bet they're all thinking, 'Hot dogs'."

He set the basket alongside two six-packs of Coors and a sack of Schuler's potato chips. A Swedish military rifle -- an AG42 B -- was concealed in an old khaki blanket under the rear seat. Fifteen rounds of 6.5 millimeter brass-jacketed cartridges in a cardboard container labeled in Swedish, kept it company.

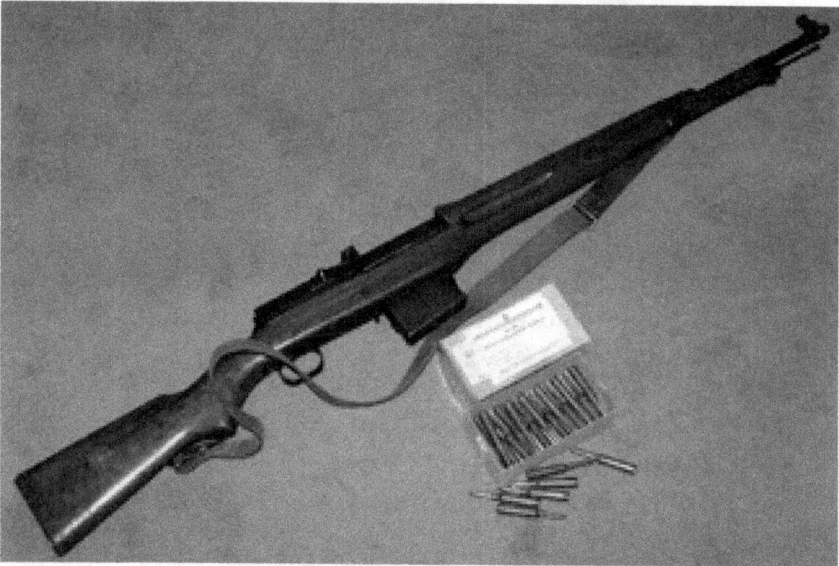

Al's grandfather brought the weapon home from Europe as "loot." He served with Patton who, according to Grampa, proclaimed, "If my men can fight across Europe, they can fuck across Europe."

Grampa confided, "I extended Patton's philosophy and stole some stuff too. He was only payin' 21 bucks a month. You should have seen all the stuff them Heinies stole."

Al backed the car out of the drive, narrowly missing Sparky, their black and white spitz, who leapt out of the way with a yelp that settled into a snarl.

"Damn, missed him again," Al laughed. He reached out the open window and pointed his finger commandingly at the dog, then shifted into first, then second and burned rubber as Sparky, yowling, poured on the gas to give chase.

"You don't like Sparky?" she said.

"He pees on my tires."

"Oh come on, it's not even your car. It's your daddy's car."

"Idiot dog!"

"Billy's got his own car. He's taking me to Saranac to eat at the hotel and see a play. He's got some good grass, too."

"Great, I hope Sparky pees the home-made paint job off that doper's heap. I might just come by and put Old Sparky in the back seat to have a go at his upholstery while you two are in the house all doped up and slobbering over each other."

"Don't you dare! So where's this picnic at, Mr. Big-Fraternity-Man?"

"Up to the Buffalo Ranch on the Blue Ridge. I think we get to ride a buffalo or something."

"That's a long way."

"We can make it in an hour. This buggy's got a lot of horses under the hood."

Al wondered, should I tell her that the fraternity picnic, with all the future hotel owners and restaurateurs, is a washout? No, better to string her along.

Of course no one else arrived at the Buffalo Company. So Al and Charlotte went through the gift shop. He hurried her to avoid buying anything.

"So where the hell is everyone?" she said as they walked out on the deck that overlooked the grazing bison. "What about all those future-big-shot hotel owners you were going to introduce me to?"

"I must have got the date wrong or maybe the rain scared them off. I don't know."

The lowering skies held back the promised rain and Al suggested his alternate plan, a trip to an old rendezvous site, the deserted iron mining village of Tahawus at the base of Mount Marcy. "Let's run up to Tahawus. We can pop some tin cans while we eat our chicken and chips. I brought that rifle I was telling you about."

"Tahawus?" she said cocking an eye and brushing back her black hair. "What you want to do at that spooky place?"

"We can shoot and, what the heck, how about a swim in one of them pits? You still got the nerve? You got your suit on underneath?"

"I got the nerve but no suit."

"Well, you never needed one before. It'll be fun. Just like old times."

123

"Not just like old times, Al. That was a mistake." She
pulled away from him toward her door and looked serious for
a moment.

Al met the resistance with the old charming smile that had worked so well on her in the past, "Come on, we're all the way out here, we got food. Let's have some fun."

"Oh shit, all right. I guess so. Let's go do something." They drove up the Tahawus Road with the Hudson on their right. Al pointed to the rocky face of the old Macintyre blast furnace, "Used to be some money made here when the mine was working. Those Macintyres took a load of money out."

"Yeah and my Daddy says their manager, the guy who did all the work, got 'accidentally' shot up here at Calamity Pond."

"Accidentally, my foot. He probably knew too much so they had him whacked."

"Yeah, probably."

They drove past the crumbling houses of the deserted village at the Upper Works, now overgrown with weed-trees and brush. Al nursed the old Cherokee around barriers and behind the rusted towering sinter plant, then over to the base of the 300-foot-high tailings pile. He stopped at the edge of the flooded strip mine, turned off the engine and reached for the door announcing, "Here we are."

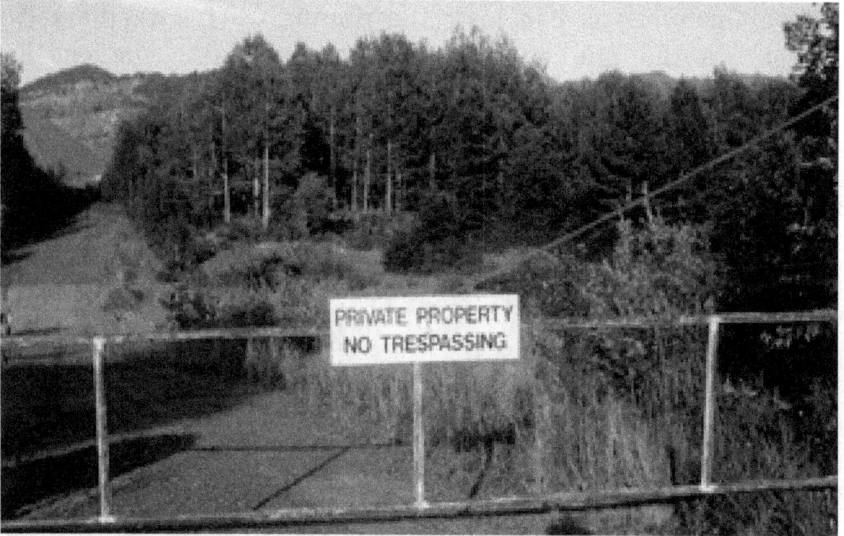

Charlotte bared her teeth, "Here? This old dump? No, let's go over to the lake. It's just over there."

Char, I like it here. The mine pit is so deep you can dive down forever, you can taste the titanium. Afterward we can climb up the pile and then maybe go inside the crusher building and find some old junk. You scared?"

"No, I'm not scared."

"Come on, I want to take a dive in the pit; see if I can touch bottom. We can go over to the lake later."

In the seclusion of the deserted mine they sat on the edge of the first pit, ate chicken and chips, drank beer. They laughed together and talked about high school dances and stealing beer from gas stations.

Then in a beery glow of sunshine and memories they went for their swim naked and slim. Dripping with cool water they stretched out on Al's old khaki blanket alongside the guarding rifle and its bullets. Al put an arm around Charlotte and she let him dry her with his tee shirt. They kissed and soon they were very close, but she struggled saying, "No, no, stop. I don't want to make that mistake again."

But Al was beyond that. He did not stop. She was strong and she struggled, but he was stronger and would not be deprived. "Stop, stop. I said stop, God damn it!" Finally, she relaxed and then responded thrust for thrust. They both finished what only he had started.

They lay together breathing hard; he dozed for a few minutes. When he awoke Charlotte was crying, "God Damn it, I'm supposed to have a date tonight."

A crab apple plunked down on the blanket.

"What's that?" she whispered, wiping her nose absently with the back of her left hand.

There was a rustling in the bushes and some laughter. Al stood up, walked over and poked around in the brush. "Some peeper I guess. Gone now."

He sat back down and wrestled with his flannel shirt till he extracted matches and a cigarette package. He smacked the pack on his knee and three popped up. He offered them to Charlotte. "Have one."

She wiped her eyes and took one. He lit it and put one in his own mouth. She inhaled deeply and blew billows from her nose.

Smiling, his unlighted cigarette close to hers, he said, "Press your burning butt to mine."

She turned away angrily and puffed as he struck a match and lit his. "What you did just now. That was against the law. I told you to stop," she said.

"Aw, come on Char, I couldn't stop. You get me going like that, how can I stop?"

"My uncle works for the Sheriff. He'll fix you," she said pulling on her jeans.

"Char, you were cooperating. I could feel it."

"I told you, No!"

"Char, Honey, don't be mad. We had a good time. What's to be mad about? Here, let's finish the beer." He yanked two cans free of the second six-pack. As they dressed, they drank generously.

Al thought, what if she takes it into her head that I forced myself on her? Now that's a ridiculous idea. She was with me all the way, pretty much all the way. But what if she gets on that high horse of hers? What if she raises some kind of a stink? How would one of those fancy law firms look at it? He glanced at the rifle and pondered.

His thoughts slipped back to a birthday party when he was seven. A little girl they called Smoochy fell into the pond in the middle of her party. All the boys were tickling her. She was going to tell. So he pushed her. Didn't they all push her? But he got the blame. There were no more party invitations till they moved. Yeah, OK, so her head hit a concrete block and she died. But she was having fun.

"Char, want to shoot some tin cans?" Al said as he picked up the AG42B and worked the bolt.

"No, I want to go home."

"We're all the way out here. I want to shoot a couple rounds. My Grampa brought this home from World War II. He stole it out of some SS officer's house."

"I'll shoot a few," she ventured.

Eyeing her cautiously, Al replied, "Yeah, OK, if you don't shoot at me."

"I promise nothing," she answered. Her smile turned down just one corner of her mouth and she tossed that black mane. Al, if he was watching carefully, might have seen a glint of fire in her eye.

They climbed to the lip of a rocky excavation. Down below, against a wall of ancient stone, were the remnants of another shooting party, broken bottles and punctured tin cans.

"We can shoot at those," Al said.

There was a shadowy spot behind a stand of sumac. He recognized the opening of a tunnel in the rock wall which he recalled from a trip here with some high school buddies.

"See that dark spot over there back of the sumac? That's a tunnel. We used to crawl in there. One place, the ceiling comes down and there's only about fourteen inches to crawl through. Crazy things kids do, huh?"

"You always do crazy things, Al. I don't know why I ever went out with you."

They sat down on the lip of the low rock cliff. He set the box of shells beside them and opened the action of the rifle. The scent of gun oil drifted up to both of them. He handed her one of the finger-length shiny brass missiles and said lasciviously, "Here, you can slide it in this time."

Unsmiling, Charlotte took the round and deftly slotted it in the chamber. Al closed the bolt, slamming the round into place nearly catching her fingertips. "Ouch," she said as she started back. He raised the rifle to his shoulder, sighted on a can and fired. The man-killing weapon spouted flame and an echoing explosive thunder that was more than either Al or Charlotte had expected. Remnants of tin went flying like an unlucky soldier's helmet.

"Good shot," Charlotte exclaimed.

"Yeah, more kick than I figured, and noisy."

A grey squirrel, alarmed by the explosion, had skittered under a bush and now poked his head out to see if it was safe to go about his business of collecting food.

"Hey, look," Char said pointing. "He's tiny. Bet you can't hit him."

Al said, "This thing would make hamburger out of him. Plus it might not be hunting season. Plus we didn't come here to kill anything."

Still, he quickly reloaded. He started to sight on another piece of tin. The squirrel had found one of those crab apples like the one that alarmed them when they lay naked. He sat up on his hind legs and twisted it about in his paws, checking it over.

Charlotte reached for the gun. "Give it to me," she demanded.

Al resisted briefly then passed the polished steel and oiled wood weapon to her. She stood up slowly, not to disturb her prey, took a pace back and raised the rifle to her shoulder. A flicker of apprehension whisked through Al as he saw the skill and ease with which she prepared the shot. But she trained the sights on the squirrel. Another great flash and roar and the little grey rodent was a blotch of red against gray rock.

Al cleared his throat and said with awe, "Very good shot."

Charlotte smiled and handed the rifle back. "I'm still going to talk to my uncle."

"Do what you got to do, just don't be shooting at me."

They traded the rifle back and forth till most of their ammunition was gone. Al had the rifle loaded and was searching over its sight for a target. Then an incoherent scream startled him. Reflexly his right index finger began a gentle precise squeeze. A man appeared over the sight. He wore tattered denim pants and jacket. His long tangled hair and beard fairly streaked behind him. He charged straight toward them, shaking a heavy stick and screaming, "You fucking, whoring, squirrel-killin' buggers, shootin' like that's a sin. Git, git the fuck out. I'll…"

For the instant before the trigger mechanism could release the firing pin Al was ten years old again. It was winter. He and Crazy Jimmy were playing by Outlet Brook just outside Lake Placid village. Teachers, parents, everyone warned the kids away from there, making it all the more attractive. Big Crazy Jimmy came running through the snow throwing chunks of ice at him, yelling, "Sissy, momma's boy, scairty cat, shit eater."

Al ran as fast as he could, not realizing that his way was blocked by water covered only by a thin layer of ice. Jimmy was about to crush him. Al suddenly dropped to his knees and threw his weight back into Jimmy's legs. Jimmy, awkward as a cow, floundered over the top of him, out onto the ice of Outlet Brook. He sprawled sliding forward and cautiously got to his feet, paused a moment as the ice began to crack, then in terror yelled "Reach me your scarf!"

Instead Al picked up a chunk of ice and threw it at him. Jimmy's face froze in horror as a crack opened beneath him and he slipped through into churning black water. Al went home, said nothing to anyone, next day in the *Adirondack Daily Enterprise* a reporter quoted Doctor Lipschutz, "The boy's body was blue ice."

A blast from the AG42B ended Al's vision. The charging wild man's head exploded and the rest of him cartwheeled over backwards.

"Are you nuts? What did you do? What did you do that for?" Charlotte screamed.

"I don't know. I thought he'd kill us," Al said quietly.

"Call the police!" she said fumbling for her cell phone.

When she had it in her hand Al reached quickly and snatched it away from her, "No, don't do that."

Al sidled over to the still form that looked like a scarecrow knocked off its perch and dumped on the ground, a pile of rags. He nudged it with the toe of his leather hiking boot.

"It's just an old bum. Tell the cops and there'll be a big stink?"

"This whole thing stinks. You went nuts and blew his head off. You raped me. You're a monster."

"The guy was coming after you, Char. You murdered his squirrel."

"Oh, now you think you saved my life? You just shot a man's head off."

Al picked up the rifle, opened the bolt and put the last of the cartridges in place. He looked at Charlotte with relaxed eyelids almost covering his pupils. For a moment the muzzle of the loaded weapon paused, pointed at the bulge of her left nipple under the scarlet fuzz of that angora sweater and then swept on past.

"What's that round for?"

He thought hard, will she screw up my life for this stupid little bitty accident? Might as well hang for a sheep they say… He swallowed and, glanced up, "It's … for that damn dog, Sparky. Next time he messes on the Jeep."

"Oh, yeah?"

"Listen Char," he said. "Please, calm down. Even though we've been making a lot of noise, no one but this bum has come around. It's a lousy day; no one knows about this but us. Who knows who this guy is? Let's think it over. You're in it as deep as me. Your prints are all over the gun. They do one of those paraffin tests on you, they'll know you fired it. I'll tell them you went off your beam when the guy caught us in the act. You plugged him, just like you did that squirrel."

Charlotte paused. "You fink!" she said, and then, "Is he dead?"

"Half his head is gone. He hasn't moved."

A halo of red oozed around the mush that should have been the scarecrow's head. It stained crimson the gray stone on which he huddled.

"Help me drag him over to that tunnel. Wait; let me see if it'll hold him. No sense spreading this mess." Al darted over the edge of the low cliff. On his hands and knees he disappeared into the mouth of the tunnel. In a few minutes, he was back dragging a soiled plaid-lined khaki sleeping bag. The leaden sky had darkened to black. A light rain began falling. Up on Marcy, thunder shook the silence.

"Good, maybe the rain will clean up the mess for us. Let's get him in this bag so we can drag him. He must have been living in there. It stinks like he's been stashing corpses."

Grudgingly, Charlotte helped get the body into the bag and together they dragged the tawdry bundle to its tomb. With effort they lifted him around behind the sumac brush that obscured the cave. Never imagining that he was assisting his murderers, the old man had also been careful to preserve that cover. Al worked the bundle far back into the tunnel and then they pushed the old man's battered belongings, including a collection of empty pop cans, back in with him.

"OK, now get out," Al whispered to Charlotte who had crowded in behind him. "I'm going to drop this roof slab. No one will ever get in here again." Charlotte scuttled out. Al backed up almost to the entrance, and working with the butt of the rifle, he loosened a slab of stone roofing from its side supports. He gave a final punch with the rifle and threw it out behind him. The roof groaned, then came down with a whoosh of dusty gravel and a resounding thump. Al rolled backward, bumping into Charlotte who blocked his way. His right foot, still in the tunnel, was hit by a flatiron-size rock. Gravel covered his leg to his knee. "Get out of the way," he yelled and fiercely worked at his ankle till he was free. He staggered to stand on his uninjured foot and found Charlotte with the rifle pointed at his belly. He shook his head. Supporting himself against the rock face, he reached into his pocket and produced the round that she had last seen put in place for Sparky.

"What's that?" she smiled, turning the rifle aside and pointing it at the ground.

"Don't point that thing at me ever again," he said.

"It's not loaded."

"You didn't know that."

"Didn't I?" she said.

He took the rifle from her with one hand and grabbed her around the waist with the other for support. "We got to get our stuff and get out of here," he said.

The rain was coming down in sheets now, lightning flashed nearby and thunder crashed simultaneously. A pitch black sky frowned down on them. Al hobbling, they picked up their spent shells and picnic remainders. Their clothes and hair matted against their bodies, wet with cold, soaking rain.

Charlotte, shivering, pointed to the spot where the old man had died. "Look."

The scarecrow's red halo was showered with cleansing rain drops. A trickle of water poured into its circle and made it a small red lake that grew and grew till it formed its own small stream that coursed over and down the low cliff, gradually diluting until there was no sign of red, no indication of the dead man at all. The little murder was washed away before their eyes.

Two weeks later, Al was at the old kitchen table that served him as a desk in his bedroom at his parents' home. He was alone. A copy of Gilbert Law Summaries lay open in front of him, a half-drained cup of sand-colored coffee beside it. A cigarette smoldered in the cup's cracked saucer. He stared at a red rose that repeated infinitely in the pattern of the wallpaper. Is she going to keep calling me like this? Can't she see what a little bitty thing it is … in comparison to the rest of our lives?

The phone in his pocket belted out its Reggae ring tone. He let it play through twice. It stopped and he took a drag on his Marlboro and a gulp of the tepid, sweet coffee. Then the now-annoying music started again. He yanked it out of his pocket, snapped it open and gave a harsh, "What?"

"It's me," Charlotte's voice rattled over the phone. "You want me to stop being your conscience; stop pestering you about the police?"

"Char, careful with those accusations."

"Then get your ass over here right now. I've got an emergency."

"And you'll get off my ass about that... little thing?"

"You get me out of this and I'll do anything."

"Anything?" he smirked.

"Get over here!"

"I'm coming." He closed the cell and slipped it into his pocket.

Al pulled on sneakers and a sweat shirt, trotted through Lake Placid's low rent district to the Forest Lake Motel. A beautifully restored '46 Chevy two-door sedan, freshly painted a metallic-fleck grey, stood in the gravel drive close to the house. As he negotiated his way past it, Sparky poked his black and white head around the side of the garage and barked.

"Shut up dog," Al muttered pointing a pistol-like finger at him. Sparky glowered and went over to relieve himself safely on the Chevy's far-side, front tire. Al rang the side doorbell.

Charlotte answered wearing another fuzzy sweater and jeans. "Come in quick."

"What's the problem?"

"Billy. He's…he's in there."

"Where?"

"In the bedroom."

"What's he doing in there?"

"We were… foolin' around."

"And?"

"He wouldn't stop. He said everyone knew I was…like that."

"Oh?"

"Yeah, I wonder who he got that from, you fucking big mouth."

Al shrugged and shook his head. "Are your folks here?"

"No. Went to Utica. We're closed. Help me get rid of him."

"Why?"

"I hit him in the head with this," and she showed Al a battered and bloody Baby Ben alarm clock that she had been concealing behind her back.

"With that?"

"I...I hit him a lot. He's not breathing"

Al and Charlotte put Billy in the trunk of his Chevy. To kill time they drove the Jeep out to Custard Mustard and Brew for a hamburger and a milkshake and went to a late movie at the Palace. They were kind of in the swing of old times so they parked on a woods road and made love in the backseat. About two a.m., they rolled Billy and his Chevy into Mirror Lake and Al walked Charlotte home.

The police, finding a plastic bag of marijuana and cigarette papers in Billy's glove compartment, confiscated half for personal use and turned the rest over to the District Attorney as evidence. The Coroner refused to get concerned over the death of a "notorious doper." And to protect the tourist trade he and the DA passed Billy's murder off to the Daily Enterprise as a "freak accident."

Epilogue

Charlotte and Al, persuaded by the statute that does not allow spouses to testify against one another, married quickly. They eventually settled in New Jersey. Now, summers, Charlotte operates a souvenir shop in the North Country; winters, she teaches NRA gun safety at a Bergen County Sportsman's Club. Al finished law school and developed a criminal defense practice in Newark.

It might be said that Charlotte and Al "Have lived happily ever after," if that can be said of any couple whose New Jersey mansion wallows on a filled swamp and whose solitary bedrooms are guarded by "His and Her" dead bolts.

FINIS

www.ingramcontent.com/pod-product-compliance
Lightning Source LLC
LaVergne TN
LVHW051640080426
835511LV00016B/2411